Cloverdale Baptist Church
Real Truth. Real Life.

IGNITING

HIS CHURCH

through

PRAYER

DR. ROB GODARD

Dedication

I come from a family that had/has a praying mom. I have no doubt that my life as a follower of Jesus was impacted by mom and dad's integrity, love for God, love for Jesus' bride, and love for us. *But*, I am convinced that one of the main reasons that I follow Jesus today is/was the prayers of my mom. Often I would come home and find her praying with an open Bible and heart devoted to Jesus. She would gather her little flock of kids at night and all of us would have to pray, and then to close. Mom would pray what felt like hours and hours of words. Her heart for God overflowed in her prayers for others. We used to bug her a little about these long prayers, or the distraction praying meant for her providing food for hungry growing boys, but I am eternally grateful that God provided me with a praying mom. *Thanks mom!*

I am thankful for my many partners in prayer, for a praying church, and for a passion to have prayer dominate our lives. Underlying all of these I know I am utterly dependent. Your prayers have allowed me to minister way beyond my potential.

Thank you for joining me in my struggle by praying for me, and may this ever increase to the glory of our King!

Contents

Introduction 9

1. Our Father in Heaven 35

2. Hallowed Be Your Name 41

3. Your Kingdom Come, Your Will Be Done 45

4. Give Us This Day Our Daily Bread 51

5. Forgive Us Our Debts as We Forgive Our Debtors 57

6. Lead Us Not Into Temptation, But Deliver Us From Evil 63

7. Revive Us 69

8. Send Us 77

9. Patterns of Prayer 83

10. The Problem of Prayer 97

11. The Pursuit a Prayer-Filled Life 101

12. The Power of Prayer in Jesus' Name 107

13. A Plan for Sharing the Gospel 109

14. Getting the Gospel Right 113

Books on Prayer 117

This book seeks to help followers of Jesus develop a pattern of prayer that can define their pursuit of intimacy with God and power to accomplish His will in this world.

I hope that you will not only read along, but that it will drive you to prayer. I hope that this will serve as a way to deepen your understanding of prayer, your intimacy with God, and your impact on His world.

I long for God's people to pray, but more than that, to know of the *pattern* Jesus has given us for prayer, so that we would experience change in our own lives, and change in the people and situations we are praying for!

> *"Man is at his greatest and highest when upon his knees*
> *he comes face to face with God."*

D. MARTYN LLOYD-JONES

Introduction

The Priority of Prayer

"We sometimes pay lip service to the delight and power of prayer. We call it indispensable, we know the Scriptures call for it. Yet we often fail to pray." J. Oswald Sanders

If only followers of Jesus would pray more, they would grow, the church would gather with more power and the world would see the beauty and glory of Jesus. Prayer is the catalyst for so much more!

I have heard (and said) that prayer is like breathing for the follower of Jesus. If that is true, there are many people who claim to be followers of Jesus who are not breathing. Without breath human life is impossible (or at the very least extremely difficult), so this is a call to breathe more, to remove the ventilator and to feel the joy of a full breath of air!

Prayer is a non-negotiable for intimacy with Jesus, for health spiritually and for impact eternally. All who call themselves Christians need to be growing in their prayer lives until they go to eternity when that prayer will become constant and indescribably deep in its intimacy. Prayer is the fire for the flame of passion and power in Christian life and ministry.

The most important reason why prayer is a priority for God's people is because Christianity is a relationship. Christians are a people of the book, who read His Word to hear from Him, and we pray to speak to Him. Like any other relationship between persons, communication is the key to growing intimacy! If someone truly has understood the gospel cognitively and responded in faith from their heart, then they enter into a reconciled relationship with the living God and one of the key ways that growth occurs in this relationship is through prayer. When those who know Jesus personally see prayer as communication, not just a shopping list of requests for a Santa-like figure, it changes how they perceive and practice prayer. Prayer is God's pathway to a deeper relationship with Him, and it is a pathway that if His followers don't walk they will find themselves weak and breathless.

Prayer is also essential for the power to live healthy spiritual lives, it is key to spiritual health. Often people who grasp the greatness of God and the smallness of humanity wonder why they should (or even can) pray to a sovereign God who rules the universe (Ephesians 1:11). Although the goal in this booklet is too small to give a thorough answer to that question, it is helpful to realize that one of the key reasons those who know Jesus are to pray is to grow in their own ability to live their lives in the world but not of the world. In fact if evangelicals were to outline keystone habits for spiritual growth, prayer always makes the top five. Prayer is about people who know Jesus conforming to His image as much as it is about them being used by Him to call on Him for help. When those who love God discover this, their longing is to know Him better as much as it is to attain His help to accomplish His purposes! When God's people pray, they spend time with Him, and when they spend time with Him they learn to conform their desires to His, and to see in their own lives answers to the prayers sent His way.

When this book walks through the pattern of prayer that God has given to His disciples, they will discover that as they seek God's best in their walk with Him, and life for Him, often the answer to their prayers is discovered in their own changes to align themselves to Him and live their lives for Him. The power of prayer is not in its pattern, but the pattern allows the person praying to have more hope for victory in their passion to pray more.

Prayer grows the follower of Jesus deeper in intimacy with Him, empowers them to become more like Him, and helps them live on mission for Him. Great revivals of first love devotion and impact for God in the sharing of the gospel almost always have come from a renewal of delight in prayer.

Prayer is one of the tools that God has sovereignly ordained to carry out His purposes for His people and His mission in the world. Prayer actually shapes the future, not because God needs anyone's prayers (for surely He does not), rather because God has chosen His children's prayers as the means by which He works in this world and their lives. That is why those in a reconciled relationship with Jesus can confidently go to Him with their requests, because the "prayers of a righteous man" can accomplish much (James 5:16). God answers the prayers of His people and moves powerfully in them and through these prayers to work in this world His will for His glory.

Literally, the prayers of righteous men and women move the hand of God. Prayer is the most an authentic Christian can do for someone else, although in this world it should never be the only thing that Jesus' followers do. Christians do not have because they do not ask—a clear indication that prayer is one of the ways that God provides for His people (James 4:2–3), and empowers them on mission for His glory.

So you should pray more! For your own sake and for the sake of the gospel, prayer must become more and more a priority for the people of God. We must become more and more a people who, "always pray and never give up" (Luke 18:1), as we pursue deeper intimacy with God and a wider impact for His glory. Brother, sister, this is an invitation to learn how to pray, but even more importantly an invitation to *pray more!*

The world has just gone through a pandemic (COVID-19) and the consequences of the response to the pandemic, and it has left many confused, fearful and angry. The isolation that is occurring has only served to increase insecurity and potential for division.

So, what should the church do? Now you might be reading this well after the pandemic is a thing of the past, but if we believe Jesus when He said, "In this world you will have trouble"[1], then in the midst of whatever

---

1.   John 16:33

circumstance you are in, the first and most important continuous thing that you should do is *pray*! COVID-19, if serious, can stop the breathing ability of the person infected and the only way to survive is through a mechanical ventilator.[2]

Always pray and don't give up![3] Prayer must become the breathing of the bride of Christ, for without it their relationship with Him will be weak, their conformity to Him woeful, and their power on mission for His glory wobbly.

Prayer is a priority for the follower of Jesus, and unless the church recovers this spark, the life of those in Canada who name the name of Jesus will be weak, and the mechanical ventilators keeping their lungs working, worn out.

The Power of Prayer

Prayer is the relational tool God has given to His people to help them accomplish His work in their lives and in the world around them. Prayer is actually the lever that moves the hand of God. Prayer is powerful and effective. The problem is that most of those who claim to be children of God have forgotten this, or been lulled to sleep in the midst of the busyness and comfort of Canadian life.

If Jesus' followers understood the power of prayer, they would pray more! It would become like breathing, with the understanding that in intense labour one might even have to think more specifically about the breathing needed.

So, to teach our hearts of the power of prayer, we will consider in this chapter stories from the Bible, promises God has made to us in His Word, testimonies found in the history of the church, and I hope, start to create a personal travel log of answered prayer.

The goal is not to just cognitively understand these stories, it is to have them grip the hearts of God's people so they know Him better and cling

---

2. In some places where mechanical ventilators were not available, other ways of helping people breathe were tried.
3. Luke 18:1

to Him in the midst of the brokenness of life. This is what God has done, and this God exists and can be set before the eyes and hearts of those who love Him.[4] He wants to be prayed to, and to provide through those prayers His power which is always enough for any and every situation!

The stories of the Bible are profound and are given to produce hope and action in the lives of the followers of God.[5] So many that stand out and, when understood to be real events in history, can be used to drive the followers of God to hope-filled powerful prayer. The God of the Bible desires to be approached, leaned on and trusted. He has displayed this in the lives of His people repeatedly and recorded it for them in His Word so that they know Him and will seek Him.

The first story comes from a time when the Israelites had just been saved. The Israelites had been a nation of slaves, having escaped Egypt through the power of God on display so wonderfully so that everyone would know He is God, and these redeemed people began their journey to the promised land. The journey turned out to be difficult and filled with problems including enemies who attacked them. They had the benefit of a great general in Joshua, however this was not enough to defeat those who were fighting them. Their resources were low, and God wanted them to rely on Him for their daily needs! Read the following slowly from Exodus 17:

Then Amalek came and fought with Israel at Rephidim. So Moses said to Joshua, "Choose for us men, and go out and fight with Amalek. Tomorrow I will stand on the top of the hill with the staff of God in my hand." So Joshua did as Moses told him, and fought with Amalek, while Moses, Aaron, and Hur went up to the top of the hill. Whenever Moses held up his hand, Israel prevailed, and whenever he lowered his hand, Amalek prevailed. But Moses' hands grew weary, so they took a stone and put it under him, and he sat on it, while Aaron and Hur held up his hands, one on one side, and the other on the other side. So his hands were steady until the going down of the sun. And Joshua overwhelmed Amalek and his people with the sword. Then the Lord said to Moses, "Write this as a memorial in a book and recite it in the ears of Joshua, that I will utterly blot out the memory

4.   Psalm 16:8
5.   Romans 15:4

of Amalek from under heaven." And Moses built an altar and called the name of it, The LORD Is My Banner. (Exodus 17:8–15)

What is happening here? Joshua is a great warrior and verse 13 tells us that he overwhelmed Amalek with the sword, and so he should be celebrated as a brave and mighty leader in war. Yet this story invites us to see the rest of the story, the hidden power of prayer. It is a story about Joshua, but he is not the main character.

The victory not only belongs to Joshua, a great warrior, it belongs to Moses who battled on the hill, and to Aaron and Hur who held his hands up seeking God's strength. In fact so strong is the message of God on the importance of prayer that he wants the Israelites and all followers of God to remember that what brought victory was not the earthly battle but the spiritual one. So hands raised in prayer caused the winning, and hands lowered the defeat. The true hero of this story is God, not Moses or Joshua, or the warriors or Aaron or Hur.

The power of prayer is so key in this victory, and the importance of praying on display, and yet that is not really the whole story. The victory, in this case, of both the people involved in prayer and the battle on the ground is to remember that victory actually is the LORD's. They were to never forget this, and to remember that the LORD is my banner.

The key to understanding this story and using it to strengthen the faith of Jesus' followers and their resolve to pray more, is to see that God is all powerful and that prayers are actually the way He works through and for His people. Arms dropping mean the battle would be lost; arms raised mean the battle would be won. There is nothing magical in Moses, or his arms, but there is something majestic in the power of prayer.

What do you believe was key in this victory for Israel? Was it Moses? Joshua? Or, deeper, was it that God's plan for the victory of His people included both Moses and Joshua, and displayed that both were utterly dependent on His strength. What do you believe is the key to victory in your own life, in the local church God has called you to build, in the mission God has called you to engage in where He has placed you in the world, but not of the world?

Maybe another read of this story with a reminder of Jesus' words in John 15, "apart from me you can do nothing"[6] would be helpful—for with Him we can do *anything*! No, really, stop reading this book, and go back and reflect on this story, in fact if you are willing, put down the book, open your own Bible to Exodus 17 and highlight this story so that it will become a part of your story, and drive you to confidently *pray more*. It is a story on prayer, on fighting in the battle where God has placed you, but even more a story on the power of God in the lives of His people through prayer. The Lord is my banner!

For the second story that displays hope and calls for prayer, there are many places that a follower of Jesus could go. They could go to Joshua (Joshua 10:1–15), and his prayers, or Elijah and the power of God that is displayed there (1 Kings 18:20–40). But for the purpose of hope in the power of prayer, against all odds, the situation in the time of Hezekiah is one of the most powerful.

> Hezekiah received the letter from the hand of the messengers and read it; and Hezekiah went up to the house of the Lord and spread it before the Lord. And Hezekiah prayed before the Lord and said: "O Lord, the God of Israel, enthroned above the cherubim, you are the God, you alone, of all the kingdoms of the earth; you have made heaven and earth. Incline your ear, O Lord, and hear; open your eyes, O Lord, and see; and hear the words of Sennacherib, which he has sent to mock the living God. Truly, O Lord, the kings of Assyria have laid waste the nations and their lands and have cast their gods into the fire, for they were not gods, but the work of men's hands, wood and stone. Therefore they were destroyed. So now, O Lord our God, save us, please, from his hand, that all the kingdoms of the earth may know that you, O Lord, are God alone." (2 Kings 19:14–19)

If you want to be amazed at the power of God and response to the prayers of His people, put down this book, pick up your Bible and read the entire story (2 Kings 18–19). Really, stop reading, put down the book, and read those three chapters of Scripture to see how hopeless situations and powerless people find victory.

---

6.   John 15:5

Let me summarize it for you. An army that no one else could stop was on the doorstep of Judah, and threatening to destroy them. It was not an idle threat as the gods of the other nations that had been attacked were useless to defend against this raiding horde. This powerful force was unstoppable, and the threat was real and overwhelming. And yet, the prayers of a humble king changed everything. God responded to the prayers of His people by assuring them of His help, and then sending the angel of the LORD to strike down 185,000 people in the camp of the Assyrians.

185,000. It may be rounded up or down a little but that is a lot of people trying to kill you and enslave your children. In a helpless situation a humble king cried out to the King, and He simply sent an angel.

God plus one is a majority, and He is more worthy of our trust and our prayers for help than anyone or anything else.[7] The pathway to praying more is worn through training our minds to acknowledge the existence of the God of the Bible and His involvement in our lives. It is so important that when those who know God are faced with insurmountable odds from a human perspective, they are almost irrelevant when God is brought to bear upon them. Like a drop from a bucket, or dust on a scale are the most powerful of human foes.[8]

It is helpful to meditate on a number of other passages in Scripture, Isaiah 40, or Psalm 46 rise to the top, but really the entire Bible is His story, and He is active in the lives of His people, and responds to their prayers. In fact He wants us to seek His face, to pray, to actively pursue His help.

For the eyes of the Lord run to and fro throughout the whole earth, to give strong support to those whose heart is blameless toward him. You have done foolishly in this, for from now on you will have wars. (2 Chronicles 16:9)

This is another story worth reading in context as it displays the consequences of not praying. But for the purpose here, notice in this verse that this all-powerful God actively pursues. He is pictured here as actively

---

7. Psalm 20:7; Psalm 9:10; Psalm 46
8. Isaiah 40

seeking those who are praying to Him to give them *strong support*. This is who God is!

God really exists. Story after story shows us that He is looking to help and able to help all who turn to Him in prayer! Pray more!

If you are a follower of Jesus, may I encourage you to highlight the dependability of God and the display of how He uses His praying people more and more as you read your Bible. You will discover that the Bible is filled with stories that glorify God and display the power of prayer, and as the Spirit works in you, these will drive up your faith and cause you to pray more. You can have full confidence in the power of prayer, for prayer is one of God's chosen pathways to release His power in the lives of His people.

The stories in the Bible are powerful faith builders, and the foundation of an effective prayer life, and so are the promises of the Bible.

When reading on prayer I often find warnings to make sure that the promises God gives us in His Word are taken in the context they are given, and I agree that this is important. The God-besotted person prays in faith following the pattern of Scripture and fully confident in the sovereignty and wisdom of God regardless of the outcome, but they should be careful not to let the correct cautions cause them to miss the call of God's Word to confident prayer. Promises should always be understood in context, and when properly understood will display the confidence those who are loved by God can have in prayer.

Here are a few of the promises that God's Word gives His followers in encouraging us to pray:

Let us then with confidence draw near to the throne of grace, that we may receive mercy and find grace to help in time of need. (Hebrews 4:16)

Is anyone among you suffering? Let him pray. Is anyone cheerful? Let him sing praise. Is anyone among you sick? Let him call for the elders of the church, and let them pray over him, anointing him with oil in the name of the Lord. And the prayer of faith will save the one who is sick, and the Lord will raise him up. And if he has committed sins, he will be forgiven. Therefore, confess your sins to one another and pray for one another, that you may be healed. The prayer of a righteous person has great power as it is working. Elijah was a man with a nature like ours, and he prayed fervently that it might not rain, and for three years and six months it did not rain on the earth. Then he prayed again, and heaven gave rain, and the earth bore its fruit. (James 5:13–18)

"Ask, and it will be given to you; seek, and you will find; knock, and it will be opened to you. For everyone who asks receives, and the one who seeks finds, and to the one who knocks it will be opened. Or which one of you, if his son asks him for bread, will give him a stone? Or if he asks for a fish, will give him a serpent? If you then, who are evil, know how to give good gifts to your children, how much more will your Father who is in heaven give good things to those who ask him! (Matthew 7:7–11)

And whatever you ask in prayer, you will receive, if you have faith. (Matthew 21:22)

You did not choose me, but I chose you and appointed you that you should go and bear fruit and that your fruit should abide, so that whatever you ask the Father in my name, he may give it to you. (John 15:16)

In that day you will ask nothing of me. Truly, truly, I say to you, whatever you ask of the Father in my name, he will give it to you. Until now you have asked nothing in my name. Ask, and you will receive, that your joy may be full. (John 16:23–24)

And this is the confidence that we have toward him, that if we ask anything according to his will he hears us. (1 John 5:14)

And whatever we ask we receive from him, because we keep his commandments and do what pleases him. (1 John 3:22)

Rejoice in the Lord always; again I will say, rejoice. Let your reasonableness be known to everyone. The Lord is at hand; do not be anxious about anything, but in everything by prayer and supplication with thanksgiving let your requests be made known to God. (Philippians 4:4–6)

Now, before you go any further, look back over these promises and highlight a few, and read them in their proper context in your Bible. Really, stop, because just reading these once will encourage you today, but the goal is much deeper and wider than that, so, slow down, take your time and drink of the promises of God until your heart is delighted and satisfied.

The better the followers of God understand the promises of God, the more they will pray confidently and in His name and in accord with His will.[9] The more those who know Jesus pray the more they will grow in their grasp of who God is, and the more they will be like Him. The more authentic Christians are like Him and grow in their grasp of who He is, the more they will pray!

So, stories in the Bible encourage relational Christians to pray, promises in the Bible show them that God answers prayer, and they can see in church history and in their own lives the joy of answered prayer. There are so many stories in church history of answered prayer, and reading Christian biography can be a huge blessing in the pursuit of growing a healthy prayer life, or in longing to pray more. Here are two more stories that I hope will encourage those who know Jesus to pray more!

Dr. Helen Roseveare, missionary to Zaire (formerly the Belgian Congo), told the following story:

A mother at our mission station died after giving birth to a premature baby. We tried to improvise an incubator to keep the infant alive, but the only hot water bottle we had was beyond repair. So during devotions that morning we asked the children to pray for the baby and for her little sister who was now an orphan.

One of the girls responded, "Dear God, please send a hot water bottle today. Tomorrow will be too late because by then the baby will be dead. And dear Lord, send a doll for the sister so she won't feel so lonely."

That afternoon a large parcel arrived from England. Eagerly the children watched as we opened it. Much to their surprise, under some clothing was

---

9. To pray in Jesus' name means simply to say we are aligning what we pray with who He has revealed Himself to be. It means we know Him as He has said He is, and we are submitting our requests to His glory. It also means that we that we are praying in His righteousness, or on His merit. An excellent resources for understanding this profound reality is Chapell's book, *Praying Backwards*.

a hot water bottle! Immediately the girl who had prayed so earnestly started to delve deeper, exclaiming, "If God sent that, I'm sure He also send a doll." And she was right! The Heavenly Father knew in advance of the child's sincere requests, and 5 months before, He had led a ladies group to include both of those specific articles.

Although many of our prayers are not answered so dramatically, God is always aware of our needs.[10]

One of the great prayer movers in the history of evangelical faith was George Mueller. He wanted normal Christians to learn to pray, and so he recorded many times where God answered his prayers with special provision. His biographies are filled with faith requests and the answers that came from God. I would encourage you to grab a biography and read it. Here is one of the many stories you could find from his life.

The captain of an ocean steamer tells that on one occasion his ship was engulfed in a dense fog off the coast of Newfoundland. It was Wednesday evening and the captain had been on the bridge for 24 hours when he was startled by someone tapping on his shoulder. He turned and saw one of his passengers; George Mueller.

"Captain," said Mueller, "I must be in Quebec on Saturday afternoon."

"That's impossible!" replied the captain. "I'm helpless!"

Mueller suggested, "Let's go down to the chart room and pray."

The captain thought he had a lunatic on board. "Do you know how dense the fog is?" he asked.

"No," came the reply, "my eye is not on the density of the fog, but on the living God who controls every circumstance of my life." Once in the chart room, Mueller got down on his knees and prayed, "O Lord, if it is consistent with Thy will, please remove this fog in 5 minutes. Thou knowest the engagement Thou didst make for me in Quebec for Saturday. I believe it is Thy will." Within a matter of minutes the fog lifted.[11]

10. Roseveare, Helen. *Living Faith.*
11. *Herald of Gospel Liberty*, Volume 102, Issues 27–52

Why did the fog lift? At least a part of that answer is the prayers of a follower of Jesus! God cares about the travel of His people—in fact, He cares about all of their cares![12]

As long as people who know Jesus can pray, they are not helpless, and the God who is sovereign over space time history uses His people's prayers to change eternity, and impact their situations. Prayer is the most important and powerful thing a follower of Jesus can do. Prayer is the best pathway to blessing others when one prays in Jesus' name, for His glory!

Do you see a need for a hot water bottle, or doll, or perhaps are in a situation filled with overwhelming odds? Pray! Pray *more*! Offer your prayers in faith, and the God of the Bible promises to answer and build your stories to encourage many others to join you in prayer!

History is full of the answered prayers of people who cast their cares on Him. I hope you remember times in your own life and ministry where God has answered your prayers and provided through them help and hope!

Often I hear people say in the midst of tragedy that they will pray, but they wish they could do so much more. Not wanting to judge the hearts of those that say this (and I have said it as well), let me say that the *most* you can do is pray, although I hope you do much more than that. Prayer is literally what the Father's children do to lift their concerns to Him and to experience His love and help.

Prayer is the most important thing a follower of Jesus can do, so if you know Him personally, *pray more*! Pray in faith[13], and the prayer offered in faith will accomplish much![14]

---

12. 1 Peter 5:7
13. Faith when used in this manner is not faith in the work, but faith in God. It includes but is not limited to a firm grasp of His *power* to do anything, His *wisdom* to always do what is right, and His *goodness* and *love* to choose that for His followers and their lives. Some have sought to make this idea of faith the focus of prayer, rather than the object of our faith, which is what the Bible calls us to have. So if you lack faith, you can gain it but getting to know the God of the Bible better, and in that understanding come to rely on Him (Psalm 9:10).
14. James 5:17; Matthew 17:20

The Preventers to Prayer

If, as we have journeyed this far together, we have discovered prayer is as important and powerful as God's Word says it is, then what is it that stops the power in prayer of those who are praying?

In fact, my guess is that if you are still reading this, you already knew at least cognitively of the power of prayer and its importance. So why have you not learned to pray more? What blocks prayer in the lives of the children of God? How can they remove those blocks so that they can accomplish the purposes of God in the power of God for the glory of God?

There is a tendency in the Canadian church to hear things as meant for others. As you read this, take the time not only to understand what might be blocking others (and yes that matters), but also what might be blocking you. If each person who claims to know Jesus will truly take the time to *pray more*, then together they will discover a significantly greater impact in and through their lives, and this will yield a healthier bride for the Groom when He returns!

In his must-read book on prayer[15], Bryan Chapell gives 10 blocks to prayer:

1. Personal Disobedience: Proverbs 28:9
2. Unconfessed Sin: Psalm 66:18
3. Unforgiving Attitudes: Mark 11:25
4. Uncaring Actions: Proverbs 21:13
5. Selfishness: James 4:3
6. Self-Promotion: Matthew 6:5–6
7. Family Discord: 1 Peter 3:7
8. Failure To Pray: James 4:2
9. Doubt: James 1:5–7
10. Community/national disobedience: Jeremiah 11:10–11

I like these, and think they are very helpful in ensuring you have removed blocks to intimacy with Jesus through prayer as you seek to *pray more*! If you want a better understanding of how to pray in Jesus' name, this is a great place to start. In fact, stop reading, and look those over again. If

---

15. Chapell, Bryan. *Praying Backwards*, pg. 181–182.

you see one you might struggle with, look up the text beside it, read it in its context and develop a strategy to move away from it so you are free to pray and powerfully impact those around you!

Here are what I believe to be the top 5 blockers of prayer in the Canadian church today.

Lethargy in Relationship

Christianity in Canada often reflects traditions rather than an intimacy in relationship. In my tradition, we say a prayer and are told we are saved. This gets the one who made the decision a get out of hell free card, and causes them to join the tradition (or if they grew up in it continue) and to go to church, camps, get baptized and embrace the church culture around which they now find themselves.

In and of themselves, many of these things are okay, even positive. The problem is that if people think they can have Christianity without a relationship with Jesus to drive and define them, they have not partaken in biblical Christianity. Traditions can actually become pacifiers, rather than the passion producers they might have been meant to be.

I think saying a prayer for salvation is healthy, *if explained well*. It is not the prayer or decision made by the individual that saves, it is confessing Jesus as Lord and believing in your heart that God raised Him from the dead.[16] The problem with a decisional Christianity is that it seems to have led to a lack of intimacy and power to live the Christian life victoriously for those who have made the choice but not found the freedom.

It is good to remind those who are followers of Jesus that He is real, that He does exist, and that those who know Him should be seeking to live their lives in a deeper more intimate relationship with Him that is founded on the gospel, and flows from the gospel to impact a passion for holiness, for obedience in all of life.

I wonder if Matthew 7:21–28 needs to be read again so that believers can wake up to the reality that Christianity is about a relationship with Jesus that drives and defines them, and in light of this relationship, that prayer is about a pursuit of intimacy with Him that delights those who know of His greatness and grace. When prayer is seen in the context of

---

16. Romans 10:9–10

relationship and communication for intimacy, it becomes much more than a discipline for godliness.

If you struggle praying, before you discipline this interaction with God into your life, make sure you truly know Him.

Review the gospel, and delight in it! Take the time to experience His love and acknowledge who you are. Confess[17] your sins and take the time to seek to live your life in a relationship with Him that is displayed by your obedience to Him. If you have said a prayer, or made a decision and joined a church, that is great and you should rejoice in those things, but don't let them hinder you from longing for so much more.

Religious people without relationship with God can pray, but never well, and their prayers are useless, and often slip into mindless repetition or manipulation techniques to get God to submit to the one praying. These prayers are not only useless and hypocritical, they become a tool of the flesh, the world and the devil in seeking to dethrone the King from the lives of people who are struggling in the brokenness of this world where humans live.

Take the time to review the gospel and rejoice in His salvation of your soul! Make a decision to follow Him, and include in that decision a longing to know Him more and to passionately live your life driven and defined by your relationship with Him. Do this daily, and as you get to know Him more, you will discover your prayer life will improve and impact!

A good way to summarize this good news is to biblically unpack the words God, Man, Christ, Response.

1. God. God is the creator of all things (Gen. 1:1). He is perfectly holy, worthy of all worship, and will punish sin (1 John 1:5, Rev. 4:11, Rom. 2:5–8).

2. Man. All people, though created good, have become sinful by nature (Gen. 1:26–28, Ps. 51:5, Rom. 3:23). From birth, all people are alienated from God, hostile to God, and subject to the wrath of God (Eph. 2:1–3).

3. Christ. Jesus Christ, who is fully God and fully man, lived a sinless life, died on the cross to bear God's wrath in the place of all who would believe

---

17. Biblical confession means more than simple acknowledgment, it means agreement. So when sins are confessed to God, it carries with it the idea of repentance, of agreement with God about those sins, and a willingness to turn from them to Him.

in him, and rose from the grave in order to give his people eternal life (John 1:1, 1 Tim. 2:5, Heb. 7:26, Rom. 3:21–26, 2 Cor. 5:21, 1 Cor. 15:20–22).

4. Response. God calls everyone everywhere to repent of their sins and trust in Christ in order to be saved (Mark 1:15, Acts 20:21, Rom. 10:9–10).[18]

Before we move on to the second major preventer of prayer, remember that sin blocks your intimacy with God, so you might be authentically saved, but struggling in sin. If you are, confess that sin to God, turn your back on it, and your face toward Him and seek to know Him more. This relational hindrance can be removed and replaced with a passion to know Him more.

The overall goal of the Christian life should be to be driven and defined by our relationship with Him, to walk like Him, to live all of our life all of the time for His glory! This pursuit will yield a life of prayer, so choose Jesus over everything and everyone else.[19]

The followers of God should live their lives in His presence, for His glory.[20] This is accomplished best in community, and the ordinances given to the church are a constant reminder of this passion for ever deepening intimacy with the Almighty.[21]

Before we move on, some don't pray because they don't realize the goodness and care of God for them individually. He does care (1 Peter 5:5) and He delights to answer, and the better we know Him through the gospel the more we will approach His throne of grace with boldness (Romans 8:32; Hebrews 4:16).

Growth in powerful prayer will always include intimacy with God through the power of the gospel and a biblical understanding of who God is in His sovereignty and immanence. So, make sure you know Him, and remove any blocks that might hinder your relationship with Him if you want to be one who changes the world through prayer.

---

18. *What is the Gospel?* 9Marks. https://www.9marks.org/answer/what-gospel/. (Some of this material has been adapted from *The Gospel and Personal Evangelism* by Mark Dever, p. 43)
19. Philippians 3:13; Luke 14:26–33
20. Psalm 16:8; 1 Corinthians 10:31
21. If you have not been baptized as a believer, or if you do not make communion a priority in your life and you claim to know Jesus, take the time to reflect on why this is. These ordinances are there to display the beauty of the gospel in symbol as well as the importance of intimacy in partaking together. These are constant reminders of the importance of living for Jesus (Galatians 2:20; Romans 6) as well as renewing your first love devotion to Him.

Laziness

It is not easy to pray. In fact, for any person who has sought to live life in a prayer-filled way, it is war! If one just prays when they are feeling like it, or it is convenient, the chances of praying more are very small!

In a nation where we believe we don't need daily bread, where our RRSPs give us retirement security, and our vacations distract us from the seriousness (and joy) of life, it is not easy to develop spiritual disciplines. Prayer is not easy, nor does it get easier.

A life of prayer takes discipline and developing a life of prayer takes time and effort. In Canada, where Christians focus more on convenience and taste than the cost and total devotion, prayer will lack.

Unlike a previous generation, few evangelicals have church prayer meetings and those that do are usually weakly attended. Prayer has taken a backseat to social justice, or doctrinal arrogance, and as such the church has lost her power.

To join the culture means to swim downstream and that is easy, to berate the culture with a small sub-culture that you gather around you is comfortable and easy, but to pray is *hard work*.

As the decisional Christianity has led to a lack of relationship, so convenient Christianity has led to a laziness, or as Piper would describe it, a lack of readiness for battle.

Until you believe that life is war, you cannot know what prayer is for. Prayer is for the accomplishment of a wartime mission. It is as though the field commander (Jesus) called in the troops, gave them a crucial mission ("Go and bear fruit"), handed each of them a personal transmitter coded to the frequency of the general's headquarters, and said, "Comrades, the general has a mission for you. He aims to see it accomplished. And to that end he has authorized me to give each of you personal access to him through these transmitters. If you stay true to his mission and seek his victory first, he will always be as close as your transmitter, to give tactical advice and to send in air cover when you or your comrades need it."

But what have millions of Christians done? They have stopped believing that we are in a war. No urgency, no watching, no vigilance, no strategic planning. Just easy peacetime and prosperity. And what did they do with the walkie-talkie? They tried to rig it up as an intercom in their cushy houses and cabins and boats and cars—not to call in fire power for conflict with a mortal enemy, but to ask the maid to bring another pillow to the den.[22]

Typical Piper, so strong, and yet something lazy content Christians must hear if we are to *pray more*!

So, choose to make prayer a priority, choose to pray as an overflow of your relationship with God, as a passion for a deeper relationship with God, as a war time weapon that the flesh and the demons can't stand against! Pray! Pray more!

Lack of Good Models

The third major reason why so many Christians are not praying as they should is that we lack good models of prayer, and maybe even given the lack of prayer meetings, or attendance at prayer meetings the opportunity to see healthy prayers happening.

Many of those who now fill the churches in Canada are people who have grown up without healthy models of prayer. This is one of the reasons that the pastoral prayer is so important in the local church—it models what healthy prayer looks like. For the churches that have shifted to a seeker-friendly model, or see the gathering of believers (church) as a place for entertainment, or outreach, prayer has shifted as a God-centred, Word-saturated war time tool, to a short inconvenient waste of time.

This is also one of the reasons that the book that transformed my own prayer life is so valuable, in modelling the prayers of Paul, through excellent exegesis.[23] In that book Carson makes the claim that one of the greatest ways to learn to pray is to watch others who know how, and follow their lead.

Families no longer pray together as they should or did, churches put prayer on the back burner, and models are few and far between for learning how to pray!

Prayer is a learned discipline, both from the Bible, and in the gathered and scattered community of faith. If the Canadian church is becoming significantly less biblically literate, and cancelling prayer modelling

---

22. *Prayer: The Work of Missions*. Desiring God. (2021, May 20). https://www.desiringgod.org/messages/prayer-the-work-of-missions.
23. Carson, D.A. *Spiritual Reformation*.

opportunities, is it any wonder that prayer is so weak, and even when it occurs, is so distant from what the Father desires!

The heart of this book will focus on learning from Jesus' pattern of prayer, which is the greatest prayer in history to follow, but the Bible is filled with prayers that we can model our prayers after, including its largest book, Psalms.

Often Canadians struggle to pray because they don't have a lot of good models from whom to learn and are lacking a biblical saturation that would include patterns from Scripture.

As a quick aside, before we get to the next block for healthy praying, if you want to learn how to pray, one of the key lesson grounds is to find someone in your church family who does this well, and join them, and listen carefully as they pour out their heart to God!

Letdown

We live in a broken world that is filled with broken people, and every life, including children of God will have trouble! Calling out to God in true prayer in your time of need is not a guarantee that what you think is best and what God knows is best will match. Many, if not all, who have cried out to God in distress, have felt the horror and pain of not having their tragedy taken away. As a pastor I can't explain why God doesn't heal the cancer of the one you love, or you live in the pain of abandonment of the one who should have loved you, or why your child would die. I don't think we get these answers until glory (usually). So what do we do when we have felt so deeply let down in life?

This is a hard one, for life is sometimes overwhelmingly difficult and tragedy strikes, and prayers are offered and left at least on the surface unanswered and the pain is sharp, deep and lasting.

If this was a book on helping people in pain the answer would be to weep with them, and when able to point them to the God who loves them and can be trusted in the deepest darkest times![24] For a solution to prayerlessness through the block of being let down, I think the answer

---

24. I have found the book *Trusting God* by Jerry Bridges incredibly simple and profound when seeking to build a strong sense of God's tender sovereignty and care for the lives of His children.

to knocking this down takes time and a focus on the greatness of God and the gospel.

God's love in the midst of crisis is the key to believing what many say to be the most precious promise in the Bible (Romans 8:32) and its context is the power of God to accomplish His purpose in all of life's confusion and pain.

So, God can be trusted, and should be reached out to, especially when we feel let down, but if you are struggling with this, allow His grace to overwhelm you even for this shortfall, and share your heart with Him. He knows it already, and He still loves you in Christ, and sometimes He will feed you[25], other times He will weep with you[26], and when you are ready, if you are truly His, He will lead you out of the wilderness and into times of refreshing once again!

The only solution to this is the gospel, and a rest in the grace and love of God, regardless of circumstances.[27]

If you have felt tremendous letdown in your life, run to God, not from Him. The great discovery of Job and so many others is that when you truly see Him your suffering may not make sense, but the clearer in focus He becomes, the less it matters. This is the lesson that Job learned and passes on to us as he reflects on His own loss and despair through incredible torment and suffering (Job 42:1–6).

We live in a broken world, and there will be times in this broken world when our pain will feel overwhelming, and our confusion debilitating. In these times, choose to cast your cares on Him, and seek to deepen your grasp of who He is! See Him as He has revealed Himself, and you will rest in Him!

Life will let you down, and even creation is groaning, so if you are looking up from the flat of your back in grief and pain, roll over onto your face and seek Him while He may be found, and in Him find rest and joy in all of life!

---

25. 1 Kings 17:2–15
26. John 11:35
27. Deuteronomy 29:29

Leadership Training

For me this was the main reason I struggled with prayer. I had been a pastor for many years, and knew the priority and power of prayer in my head. But every time I started to pray, my mind would drift to the business of my day or the loss the Canucks had suffered the night before. I had never been trained to pray (outside of the powerful model of my mom). So although I knew its importance, I did not experience its power.

Sadly this mind drift did not find its way back to prayer and often, even with good lists I felt like giving up. Soon prayer was something that I did professionally but not personally and this terrified me.

The pathway out for me included learning how to journal and growing in my understanding of relationship with Jesus, but perhaps the most important discovery I made was to learn from experts how to pray.

Their pattern was a blessing for me, and learning to follow their pattern gave me a way to pray in the Spirit that was sure and true. The book that most impacted my life in this (and one we make sure every elder of our church has in their quiver) is Carson's, Spiritual Reformation. I have since made training in prayer an important topic in my training of other pastors, and taught on it as a specific subject for seminarians. If the evangelical world does not train its leadership to pray, it should not be surprised that God's people in their care struggle with this.

So what is a simple yet life-changing pathway forward? To start, I would suggest to look at each of the blocks we walked through and to honestly ask yourself if this is blocking your prayer life.

- Lethargy
- Laziness
- Lack
- Letdown
- Leadership

Some might be beyond your control, but make sure specific blocks to your own life are taken care of, and the rest of this book will try to take care of the last one, and offer some training in the pathway that Jesus has left us to pray.

Let us now join the disciples, and go to the Master Teacher, and ask Him, "Lord, teach us to pray."

The Pattern of Prayer

This is where the rubber hits the road! This is the *so what?* time, the practical focus that seeks now to start down this pathway of praying more. Lord Jesus, our Master, and the One whose life so shines in this relationship, *teach us to pray.*

"Beware of practicing your righteousness before other people in order to be seen by them, for then you will have no reward from your Father who is in heaven.

"Thus, when you give to the needy, sound no trumpet before you, as the hypocrites do in the synagogues and in the streets, that they may be praised by others. Truly, I say to you, they have received their reward. But when you give to the needy, do not let your left hand know what your right hand is doing, so that your giving may be in secret. And your Father who sees in secret will reward you.

"And when you pray, you must not be like the hypocrites. For they love to stand and pray in the synagogues and at the street corners, that they may be seen by others. Truly, I say to you, they have received their reward. But when you pray, go into your room and shut the door and pray to your Father who is in secret. And your Father who sees in secret will reward you.

"And when you pray, do not heap up empty phrases as the Gentiles do, for they think that they will be heard for their many words. Do not be like them, for your Father knows what you need before you ask him. Pray then like this:

"Our Father in heaven,

hallowed be your name.

Your kingdom come,

your will be done,

> on earth as it is in heaven.

Give us this day our daily bread,

and forgive us our debts,

> as we also have forgiven our debtors.

And lead us not into temptation,

> but deliver us from evil.

For if you forgive others their trespasses, your heavenly Father will also forgive you, but if you do not forgive others their trespasses, neither will your Father forgive your trespasses.

"And when you fast, do not look gloomy like the hypocrites, for they disfigure their faces that their fasting may be seen by others. Truly, I say to you, they have received their reward. But when you fast, anoint your head and wash your face, that your fasting may not be seen by others but by your Father who is in secret. And your Father who sees in secret will reward you. (Matthew 6:1–18)

Stop—read that again, and ask Jesus to teach you how to pray! His Spirit uses His Word to teach His children, and we should start and stay there in our growing process!

Jesus begins with a warning, or a negative. It is focusing on two dangers that He thought would distract His disciples—don't pray like hypocrites, and don't pray like pagans.

The hypocrite wants to be seen by man as super spiritual. This is the person who keeps the *thee's* and *thou's*, and is loud and in the front and centre of the noise. This is the person who fasts in public and wants everyone to know they are fasting, and misses the point of following the words of Jesus.

In private they rarely pray, but in public, their prayers are deep and theological (at least in their own minds). They pray to and for man, and miss the Master completely. To say, don't be like the hypocrites, really is to acknowledge that God is real, that your relationship is with Him, and although it includes others, it focuses on God. Authentic followers of Jesus seek Him, and His approval and eternal treasure, not the pleasures of man.

It might be helpful to pause here and again ask the question, "if you really believed that God was real, and listening to you, how would that change your prayers?" How would it change how you approach God and with what you approach Him? It is important to Jesus that we don't slip into the religiosity of public prayers for the people, but actually practice His presence. Pray to the Father, through the Son, in the power of the Spirit, not to the people in the power of your personal righteousness! Not only do hypocrites receive their reward in full, they are in danger of adjusting the gospel and receiving the wrath of God (Galatians 1:10). People pleasing religion is dangerous and damning!

Jesus warns against man-centredness, and He also warns that His followers should not be like the pagans. The pagan thinks that by the use of words, and the repetitive nature of his mindless prayer he will be heard by God. This person is deceived, and does not understand what it means to know the God of the Bible. He is not impressed with our bargaining, or our mindless mantras, He wants our hearts overflowing, and our intimacy growing!

Once Jesus has dealt with the negative, He shifts to the pattern, and this is the helpful pattern we want to see produced in heart felt, cognitively engaged prayer. So our format will change a little, and shift to encouraging you to not only learn, but to live that out. To understand the pattern that Jesus wants you to follow and then to actually begin your journey, or continue it, book in hand.

Prayer is not informing God, it is relating our needs to God. It is an opportunity of intimacy and dependence. He loves to hear the prayers of His people.

This prayer is broken up into six requests, the primary one being for God's name to be Hallowed, and the rest an overflow of radical God-centredness that is displayed in absolute dependence and submission. Many have also observed correctly that the pattern begins with three requests that are radically God-centred, and then the last three focus on the children of God's physical, emotional and spiritual needs. This is not a prayer you jump into, it is relational and radical, and if followed as a pattern will not only teach you how to pray it will change eternity. The prayer requests are not only for others, but ones that can be personally applied and grown in. So let us learn and follow the pattern of prayer given by the Person of Jesus.

Following the Pattern

"The Lord's Prayer is without a doubt the greatest prayer of the Christian church."[28] Please take the time with me to learn the content and follow the path. My hope is that you will learn this in community and apply it

---

28. Hughes, Kent. *Abba Father*, pg. 13

with other Christians from your local church. That together you will follow this pattern and that it will impact the way you pray, and that together and alone you would pray more!

This next section is designed to be used to help God's people to follow Jesus' pattern and to pray more. My prayer is that those reading this will not only desire to pray more, and have learned more about prayer, but to actually engage in more effective and powerful prayer. Please take the time as you walk through this book to actually pray. To learn about, and apply. It is also a portion written to encourage local churches in corporate prayer. To give a model, so that God's people will pray more together. May God choose to use this to hallow His name, and build His Kingdom through the prayers of His faithful children.

1

Our Father in Heaven

Our

Notice that this pattern for prayer is plural. This does not mean that you can't pray alone, but it does mean that God has called us to pray as a part of a community! He is *our* Father. We are brothers and sisters, and the very way that this prayer starts is that God is our Father is an amazing privilege that should overwhelm us. We are unified in Him, and through Him we love one another as spiritual family.

Those who know Jesus as Lord and Savior become a part of a much larger family, the universal Church that includes all Christians from all of history and right now, and as precious, a part of a local church where the love of God can work through the people of God for the glory of God.

Make sure to pray with your family, especially those from the local church that God has privileged you to serve. The local church is a key priority for those who have experienced the power of the gospel, and it is

God's plan A to conform people to His image, and reach the world with His gospel (and there is no plan B).

Father

This is a familiar word of intimacy and respect. As far as we know, "there is no evidence of anyone before Jesus using this term to address God"[1]. This is the name Jesus called God in prayer every time He prayed but one.[2] It makes sense for Jesus to address His Father this way, but for those who were a part of Israel's faith community it was foreign and much too familiar. God longs to be treated as holy, as we shall see soon; however, we should run to Him and cling to Him and know Him as our dearest Father.

It is a shocking way to address the One who is in heaven and shows the tender love and care of God for us! Almost all prayers in modern evangelical churches begin with this reference to God, and yet so few acknowledge the profound reality that it displays about our relationship with the God of the Universe. The One and Only True God cares about us as our Father. He knows my name! He loves me as His child. The sovereign Ruler of the universe cares about my little life. This is overwhelming and life changing and if realized in the heart will drive the children of God to constant prayer. He is personal and caring. Packer states:

> You sum up the whole of New Testament religion if you describe it as the knowledge of God as one's holy Father. If you want to judge how well a person understands Christianity, find out how much he makes of the thought of being God's child, and having God as his Father. If this is not the thought that prompts and controls his worship and prayers and his whole outlook on life, it means that he does not understand Christianity very well at all. For everything that Christ taught, everything that makes the New Testament new, and better than the Old, everything that is distinctively Christian as opposed to merely Jewish, is summed up in the knowledge of the Fatherhood

---

1. Carson, D. A. *Matthew*, pg. 169.
2. Matthew 27:46

of God. 'Father' is the Christian name for God. Our understanding of Christianity cannot be better than our grasp of adoption."[3]

A good translation of this would be, "our Dearest Father"—intimate and respectful. Knowing who He is, and that He loves us as His children is the pathway into prayer. This way of addressing the One we pray to reminds us of His care for us, and that we can have confidence that He will give good gifts to His children![4]

Prayer at its core is relational. Could it be that one of the reasons that the Canadian church lacks a concerted and constant pursuit of God in prayer is because we have forgotten this?[5] Our *dearest Father* loves us, and has forgiven us. This prayer is corporate, relational, intimate and reverent.

In Heaven

This reminds us that He is sovereign and over all things. He is a God you can know personally and intimately (Father), and a God you can trust completely (He is over all!).

Father = Immanence   In Heaven = Transcendence

We approach the throne of grace with boldness, and reverence knowing He loves us and has power over all things. When we enter into His presence, let us do so joyfully and reverently. Confidently and with care. We cling to Him, we run to Him, aware He is over all and sovereign and delighted that He notices His children and loves them, and cares about their lives. (Isaiah 40; Psalm 115:3; Job 1:21–22; 2:10)

---

3.   Packer, J. I. *Knowing God.*
4.   Matthew 7:11
5.   Galatians 4:6; John 1:12; Romans 8:15–16

Prayer

Our dearest Father in heaven. You love me, you are concerned about my welfare, and care so much more than any human good father. Thank you for loving me as your child. Thank you for so great a salvation that allows me to call you dearest Father, and rejoice in the intimacy of your love and grace. You are in heaven, you are sovereign over all things, and the creator and sustainer of life. You are all powerful and trustworthy. Thank you that I can trust you in the tenderness of your care and the power of your hand.

Take a moment to write this phrase Jesus taught His disciples to pray in your own words:

Prayer Notes

- Adoration: Focus on who God is: His attributes.
- Confession: Agree with God on your sins and turn your back on them and your face toward Him.
- Thanksgiving: Start with the gospel and then thank Him for every good and perfect gift.
- Supplication: He wants to hear from your heart specific things you want Him to engage in.

2

Hallowed Be Your Name

Hallow

This is the core prayer request that is centred on God and how His name is viewed by His children and the world. Hallow means to sanctify, to set apart. Here, it is a reference to His infinite greatness, His uniqueness, His absolute purity. When we pray, hallowed be your name, we are asking God to:

- Use our lives to show how holy holy holy He is.
- Have others know Him and hallow Him as well.

In essence it is a prayer that God's name would be glorified. That God would be *treated as holy*. That He would be known for who He has revealed Himself to be and treated with the respect and reverence He deserves because of who He is.

Name

Name: the sum of who you are, a representation of your being. Those reading the New Testament would have understood that when someone's name is being referred to, it is a reference to their character, to who they are. So in this case, when children of the Father pray that God's name is hallowed, they are praying that who He is would be known, and treated with reverence. "God's name is a reflection of who He is. God's name is God Himself as He is and has revealed Himself, and so His name is already holy."[1]

So this primary and all-encompassing prayer request is that God would make His Name (who He has revealed Himself to be) supreme in all of His children's lives, and the life of the every other living human. In fact perhaps beyond that to all of the universe for all eternity! This prayer to God is that those who know Him would realize who He is and reflect that Holiness as His followers and that others would choose to do this with us because of their prayers and lives!

"How is God's name hallowed amongst us? Answer: When our life and doctrine are truly Christian."[2] "God's name is reverenced when we live lives that reflect Him."[3] (Piper sees this request as the most important of all of the requests in Jesus' pattern for His people to learn how to pray. Most people break up the prayer into three God-centred requests, three for ourselves. Piper would see this as one and then five ways to accomplish this, seeking for all to be God-centred).

To pray this prayer (and have it answered in our lives) we must be constantly growing in our biblical understanding of who God is (name) and in living our lives in obedience to His Word. We want our lives to reflect who He is, and to have others do the same (1 Corinthians 10:31). (Psalm 20:7; Isaiah 6:1–11; Psalm 9:10)

---

1. Carson, D.A. *Matthew*, pg. 170.
2. Martin Luther
3. Hughes, Kent. *Abba Father*, pg. 34.

Prayer

Our dearest Father, the sovereign Ruler of all, who is in Heaven, may you be known as Holy, as set apart, as the One who is supreme and pure. Please help me to know your holiness and to live in such a way that my life displays who you are to others. Please would you bring about a clarity to your Person that would create a massive response of worship and submission from your people and beyond. You are holy holy holy. May we see you, and in awe live for your glory, so that through this prayer and our lives, your name will be hallowed.

Take a moment to write this phrase Jesus taught His disciples to pray in your own words:

Prayer Notes

- Adoration: Focus on who God is: His attributes
- Confession: Agree with God on your sins and turn your back on them and your face toward Him.
- Thanksgiving: Start with the gospel and then thank Him for every good and perfect gift.
- Supplication: He wants to hear from your heart specific things you want Him to engage in.

3

Your Kingdom Come, Your Will Be Done

This is a prayer for absolute and total submission to God, not only offering the lives of the people praying, but also the lives of those they are praying for.

Your Kingdom Come

The Kingdom of God (or heaven if the concept is drawn from Matthew) is synonymous with His rule.

He is *King*. He is the ruler over all!

Kingdom = God's Reign and His Will.[1]

He is ruling now in the lives of His children. He will rule for eternity fully and completely. This is an extension of the first request of hallowing God's Name in that the primary way of hallowing God's name is to obey His Word.

---

1. Kevin DeYoung

Therefore His Kingdom has an *already-and-not-yet* component. Already there are those submitting to His Kingship (albeit not perfectly), and in eternity He will be submitted to fully and completely! He is King, He is the returning King, He will reign forever!

So this prayer is not only an acknowledgement of His Kingship in the life of His children, it is a prayer for Jesus' return where God will be displayed in the beauty of His rule to all! *Even so, Lord Jesus come!*

Your Will Be Done

This is a prayer request for God's will to be followed, His Word known and obeyed by His people, and that through their impact on the world, they would display His beautiful gospel.

God's will is understood best in two key ways:
- Decree: What He is working out in all things: Romans 8:28–29; Ephesians 1:11; Matthew 10:29–30
- Desire: What He commands in His Word[2]

This is a prayer for submission to God and His Word. This is asking for the reign and rule of God now in the hearts of people, offering themselves first and foremost to full obedience, but also longing for this in others. It is an evangelistic and Lordship prayer, longing for the return of Jesus. It is a prayer of full submission, and longing for others to join us in this radical whole hearted obedience.

Your children submit to you, God, and they long to live on mission for you so others will submit to you as well! Help us to do your will with joy and absolute obedience! This prayer implies a life of repentance and full devotion to Jesus and obedience to His revealed will and a constant adjustment of how His subjects think, feel and act to what God has revealed for them to do in love. (Matthew 28:16–18; Matthew 4:17; 7:21–27)

---

2. R.C. Sproul adds a third, His disposition, meaning what is pleasing or displeasing to Him (*The Prayer of the Lord*, pg. 55).

This is not only something His children should pray for, it is something they should pursue (Matthew 6:33). This is pursued through Word saturation, passionate obedience and willing gospel living and sharing. This is something those ruled by the King long to see happen in others as they submit to God's good rule through their lives and lips. In many ways this is a discipleship prayer, longing for people to obey all that God has commanded them.

> These first three petitions, though they focus on God's name, God's kingdom, and God's will, are nevertheless prayers that He may act in such a way that His people will hallow His name, submit to His reign, and do His will. It is therefore impossible to pray this prayer in sincerity without humbly committing oneself to such a course.[3]

3. Carson, D.A. *Matthew*, pg. 170.

Prayer

Our dearest Father, sovereign over all things as You are in heaven, you are the King of kings and the Lord of lords. You have the right to rule, and You rule. You are my King, and as such I submit my life to You as my Sovereign. I long for you to rule over others here on earth, so please would you open the eyes of people to see how majestic you are, and would they submit to you as King. Your will is my desire, and I pray that your will would be done in my life, and in those around me. That there would be a delight in you and a desire for full obedience. Please work this in me, and forgive me for when I fall short. Help me to live my life in joyful submission to you as my King, Ruler, and Master!

Take a moment to write the this phrase Jesus taught His disciples to pray in your own words:

Prayer Notes

- Adoration: Focus on who God is: His attributes
- Confession: Agree with God on your sins and turn your back on them and your face toward Him.
- Thanksgiving: Start with the gospel and then thank Him for every good and perfect gift.
- Supplication: He wants to hear from your heart specific things you want Him to engage in.

4

Give Us This Day Our Daily Bread

The pattern of prayer that Jesus has given to His disciples now turns from praying for God's glory, to relying on Him to provide for them and work in them so that He will be glorified and they will be satisfied. This should (and must) be a prayer they pray for themselves, and this prayer shows us how Jesus' model patterns this. This is a prayer of dependence upon God for all of His children's needs. This is an acknowledgement of utter and total dependence, and that God is dependable.

Give Us

This is a prayer of utter dependence, and realizing that every good an perfect gift is from Him.[1] Those who call Him Father acknowledge that they need Him even for their most basic needs.

---

1.   James 1:17; John 15:1–11

This Day

This is a prayer that reminds His children of their daily moment by moment need for God to provide for them. Even the ability to provide comes from Him. All humans are utterly dependent on God for everything, even when their storage barns are full! This is a reminder of what most Canadians need to hear in terms of the independent living patterns they are following.

Some translations talk about the word "day" as being extremely difficult to translate, and might even refer to tomorrow's needs, but the idea is dependence on God for short term physical needs. *We are utterly and completely dependent on him!* It is a dependence that would have reminded those familiar with the Old Testament of God's care for His people with manna every day, available for His people as they journeyed toward the promised land.

As God's children journey through this life, they can and must rely on Him for their needs. He wants to be relied upon, and if His children are to attain full dependence and His sufficiency, He must be relied upon.

The danger of self-sufficiency was real for the Israelites and is real for the Canadian church. This is a longing that we would know our great need, and His willing provision. (Deuteronomy 8:17)

Our Daily Bread

Most scholars would argue that this phrase refers to "all of our physical needs."[2] God cares about small things, and providing them for His children. He wants to be asked, and to be seen as the provider of our needs. In an age of massive self-sufficiency (or at least the hypocrisy of thinking we have it) the fact that this is a daily provision request makes this a daily reminder of our utter dependence on Him for everything, especially focused on here, everything in the physical world where we live!

---

2.   Carson, D.A. *Matthew.* Pg. 171.

Prayer

Our Dearest Father, thank you for knowing our lives well and loving us. It is a joy to be your child. Father, you are in heaven, you are sovereign over all things, your power has no limits, and no one can stay your hand. You are accomplishing your will and we can trust in you! You are the King of all, and I am yours fully. I surrender my life to you again, and ask that your rule would be on display in my life and that you would use me to help others to know you and submit to you. Your will be done perfectly in my life, as I long to obey always, and would you help me to build this into the lives of others as well. Please help our church family to succeed in teaching people to obey all that you have commanded.

Would you please help us to remember that we are completely dependent on you for all things! You are dependable and we need you desperately. Please provide for us, for our physical needs every day, and help us to live in active and passionate dependence on you. Apart from you we can do nothing and with you, we can do all things. Thank you for providing for us![3]

Take a moment to write the this phrase Jesus taught His disciples to pray in your own words:

---

3.   Romans 8:32; Matthew 10:29–31

Prayer Notes

- Adoration: Focus on who God is: His attributes
- Confession: Agree with God on your sins and turn your back on them and your face toward Him.
- Thanksgiving: Start with the gospel and then thank Him for every good and perfect gift.
- Supplication: He wants to hear from your heart specific things you want Him to engage in.

5

Forgive Us Our Debts as We Forgive Our Debtors

The first three petitions in this prayer are not linked other than in their being God-centred, but the last three are linked with a connector (and). This shows that physical provision from God, as His disciples depend on Him is not enough.

They need more to function in a healthy way while here on earth! Their prayer should never be limited to the physical needs they have. It should also include their spiritual needs (in fact Paul's prayers seem to model this passion well, and focus intensely upon the spiritual).

Forgive Us Our Debts

God's children need spiritual health, and relational forgiveness from God is essential to an intimate relationship with the Living God! (1 John 1:9) Jesus' forgiveness in terms of eternal punishment is once for all, at conversion (Romans 8:1; 2 Corinthians 5:21). But His followers must keep a short list of accounts when it comes to confessing their own sin to keep their relationship with Him strong, and their growth in conformity to Him healthy!

Jesus' disciples should live lives of repentance before their God, which means to constantly align themselves with His Word and His person, and confess to Him where they fail.

Remember as a part of this prayer, His followers should seek to experience His real forgiveness and the relational intimacy from this so that they can fight the accusations of the enemy who wants to hold them in their sin and in condemnation. (Psalm 103:12)

It is also important to remember that confession of sin is agreeing with God (God's Word) about behaviour, not just reciting what has been done. It comes not from the heartache of being caught, but from the longing to be right with God. God's children will always need forgiveness until heaven, for even their best is as filthy rags (Isaiah 64:6), and God is *holy* (Isaiah 6:1–7). Pursuing this removal of blocks from intimacy with God will always include confession of all known sin for those who are seeking to live life before the face of God.

As We Forgive Our Debtors

Experiencing God's forgiveness makes His followers those who will forgive others of their sin, recognizing that the debt to God is massive, and the debt that others have towards them through their sin is substantially less (not even worth comparing)[1].

---

1. Matthew 18:15–35

Spurgeon said, "Unless you have forgiven others, you read your own death-warrant when you repeat the Lord's prayer."[2] Those are pretty strong words, and worth reflecting on.

If you struggle forgiving someone else when they have sinned against you, don't bask in self-pity or condemnation—fix your eyes on Jesus and long to experience the richness of His forgiveness, because only then will you be able to forgive (2 Corinthians 5:14). The pathway to forgiving others is to recognize the glory of the gospel in your own life! Pray Ephesians 3:14–21 if you struggle forgiving others, and keep your focus on Jesus!

---

2.   Spurgeon, C.H. *Forgiveness Made Easy* (January 1, 1970).

Prayer

Search me, O God, and see if there be any impure way in me. Help me to know your word and align myself with it. Please forgive me for my sins (be specific as the Spirit brings this to mind)_____, and help me to experience this forgiveness so richly that I forgive others of their sin towards me!

I long to experience your love, and to align my life with your grace so richly that I live this life of grace in light of all that happens to me.

Take a moment to write the this phrase Jesus taught His disciples to pray in your own words:

Prayer Notes

- Adoration: Focus on who God is: His attributes
- Confession: Agree with God on your sins and turn your back on them and your face toward Him.
- Thanksgiving: Start with the gospel and then thank Him for every good and perfect gift.
- Supplication: He wants to hear from your heart specific things you want Him to engage in.

6

Lead Us Not Into Temptation, But Deliver Us From Evil

The Christian life is a call to battle, against the world, the flesh, and the devil. God is the only One that can keep His children from temptation, and so they enter into this battle for holiness and gospel impact asking for His deliverance. In the spiritual realm, the demonic realm is much stronger than the human, but God protects His own, and the evil one cannot harm them.[1]

When it comes to the spiritual battle that is real and intense, Christians in history have either slipped into the ditch of complacency, ignoring the reality of the battle altogether or of fear, giving more credit to the power of the demonic, and less to the omnipotent God of the Bible. It is important for children of God to recognize that they are in a spiritual battle, and to stay out of the ditches of complacency or fear, by going to God in confident prayer.

---

1. 1 John 5:18

Lead Us Not Into Temptation

"Don't allow us to come under the sway of temptation that will overpower us and cause us to sin." This request includes a protection from trials (same Greek word) that would take the focus of the follower off Jesus. It also includes a realization that their life goal is to conform to the image of Jesus and to reach others for Him.

Humans are profoundly weak and need God's help, especially in their spiritual battle (2 Corinthians 12:10). If God was to withhold His tender care, the demonic realm would destroy and kill them, but in His tender care they cannot do more than He allows, and all God allows is for the good of His children and the glory of His name.

If God was to withhold His grace, the flesh would fall into temptation, sin, and destruction. God's work in salvation is awe inspiring and He continues to work in His children to protect and finish what He started (Philippians 1:6). Every child of God is a trophy of grace, and God's grace will be on display in their stories for all eternity (Ephesians 2:7).

The world that humans inhabit is a spiritual world, and as such followers of God must be ready to battle spiritually (Ephesians 6; Matthew 4; Genesis 3). The first step in this is dependent prayer. This battle impacts every area of life, and is something God's followers must have God's help with or they will fail.

Deliver Us From the Evil

Some translations differ—"deliver us from the evil one"—same idea. There is a battle against the demonic realm that we all must face. This battle is real, and one that must be fought from strength in the Lord. The Devil is a real person, and evil exists, and in this broken world impacts all who live in the world. Only God can deliver us from this evil, and from the evil one and his minions.

Take heart, for God is *greater* (Isaiah 40; 2 Corinthians 12:1–10; Job 1–2—especially 1:21–22, 2:10). In this struggle against the demonic realm, followers of God must remember their dependence on Him, and display this in their prayers to Him!

The pathway to victory for Jesus' disciples is paved in a pursuit of a prayer-filled life, and a God-besotted sight. The better followers of God know Him, the more effective they will be at experiencing His power in their pursuit of holiness and impact in the world for His glory. (1 John 5:18; 2 Corinthians 12:1–10)

Prayer

Father, I want to live my life for you, pure and holy, and on mission. I know I am in a spiritual battle, so I ask you to help me to fight off temptations, and to be strong in trials to show how great you are! Please protect me from the evil one and his schemes, and help me to keep my eyes on you and your power and grace. I am confident in your protection, and trust you in all that life brings my way. I will seek to use every experience to display your holiness through mine, and your gospel to all who see me in trials and in spiritual battle.

Take a moment to write the this phrase Jesus taught His disciples to pray in your own words:

Prayer Notes
- Adoration: Focus on who God is: His attributes
- Confession: Agree with God on your sins and turn your back on them and your face toward Him.
- Thanksgiving: Start with the gospel and then thank Him for every good and perfect gift.
- Supplication: He wants to hear from your heart specific things you want Him to engage in.

If you grew up quoting the Lord's prayer there is a good chance you closed it with the words, "For thine is the kingdom, and the power, and the glory, for ever. Amen."[2]

Almost all scholars agree that this was not in the original manuscripts (it is left out of all of the oldest available to us), and that it was used by the early church consistently. This phrasing is found in the Didache, and is helpful in practice in terms of keeping this prayer radically God-centred. Because it is not in the original manuscript, we will not include it in this study, but the pattern of the New Testament church is helpful to keep His children radically God-centred and help them to remember that Jesus is *the King*, and all of their lives are to seek His glory! It reminds disciples of who He is and what He is capable of doing in our lives.

- The Kingdom = God is *King*
- The Power = God is *all powerful*
- The Glory = We are to live our lives for His glory!

It is a reminder of God-centredness—where this prayer started.

---

2. Matthew 6:13 (KJV)

7

Revive Us

*If my people who are called by my name humble themselves, and pray
and seek my face and turn from their wicked ways, then I will hear
from heaven and will forgive their sin and heal their land.*

2 CHRONICLES 7:14

The Lord's prayer is the perfect pattern for the people of God who want
to learn how to pray. There are many other patterns and calls to prayer in
the Bible that should not be forgotten, including almost the entire book
of Psalms and much of the New Testament.

As this book is written to cause God's people to *pray more*, and to
follow patterns in Scripture, this content is a call to pray for revival.

The church in Canada is in trouble. It is small, and worldly. It is
shrinking and discouraged. It is filled with people who don't act lovingly
or truthfully online, though perhaps they are a little softer when in the
actual presence of other people. It is divided and failing, and yet, Jesus has
promised to build His church. So to those who attend local churches, and
hear about what is going on in the greater evangelical church world, this is
a call for personal powerful revival in their own lives, as well as a call to pray
for others to experience the richness of full unbridled devotion to God.

The most important thing that we can do in a time of trouble is *pray*! This is a time of need for the Canadian church, so those who are authentic in the church must approach the throne of grace with boldness to find help in this time of need.[1]

2 Chronicles 7:14 is a promise made to Israel by God at the completion of the temple. Although it is not directly applicable to Christians in Canada, it is certainly a promise that shows them the pathway that God looks for in His people when they are struggling with apathy or legalism, when they long for His presence and power in their lives and for impact in the world where God has placed them.

So, as a part of the Canadian church, what can we do now to display our dependence, and pursue His power for renewal and revival? We remember that this verse in its context is for Israel, and it displays the power of God for them as a nation. We also know that it shows us His pattern, and gives us hope, so we take this verse to heart, not to save Canada as a nation, but to empower Canadian Christians to have a first love devotion, and to impact their world with the gospel of Jesus. Take this verse to heart:

If My People Called by My Name

This is for God's children, who know who He is and long to be like Him. Yes, specifically to Israel as a loyal nation, but by extension, we can learn from this pattern a healthy way to approach God in our time of need for His strength and power for revival.

1. Humble Themselves

Humility is the only right approach to God. C.S. Lewis profoundly defined humility, explaining that it is not thinking less of yourself, but thinking about yourself less.[2] In this case it includes an acknowledgement of who God is, and who the person praying is. This means a sight of God's power,

---

1.   Hebrews 4:16
2.   Lewis, C.S. *Mere Christianity*, Book 3, Chapter 8, "The Great Sin"

wisdom, and holiness, and from this a reflection on the weakness, sin, and lack of knowledge of the person praying.

It is powerfully seen in Job at the end of his ordeal (Job 42:1–6) and in all who are truly seeking to know God. Humility comes from seeing God as He has revealed Himself to be, and from that truly becoming aware of who we are. It includes the reality that, "apart from [Him] you can do nothing"[3], but it is more than that, it is an exclusive and full focus on God and His word and will, overflowing from an acknowledgement of being poor in spirit. It is a choice to see God, and know oneself. It is a feeling of the powerless relating to the *all powerful*, and rejoicing that He is for us.

2. Pray

This is active pursuit of God's presence relationally for the situations that are brought to Him. Simply put it is communicating with God. The humble will seek His face, and bring their requests to Him. Those longing to know Him more, live for Him with more impact and conformity, and love those around them His way will *pray more*.

I think it is helpful to note that this is a corporate movement that is praying, and although individuals must pray, this is a corporate prayer from God's people longing for their first love devotion to be restored and His power to be displayed. God's people who have humbled themselves must pray!

3. Seek My Face

Seeking God's face is an active pursuit of His presence and favour. It is a seeking to live life in the reality that He exists, and His Word is true. So many Canadian Christians have lost sight of this, and live as though He does not exist. Ignoring Him, or His omnipresence, is where sin can overwhelm and become a pattern of life. This seeking of God's face is an emphasis and reminder on seeking God's presence in all of life. It is focused on three key realities.

- The God of the Bible truly does exist. He is who He says He is.
- It is a seeking of His presence that is practical and impacts how the child of God feels, acts and thinks. It includes a desire to live life as

---

3.   John 15:5

though He exists because He does. In this it is a desire for intimacy with the Almighty. It is a longing to know Him, and to set Him before you (Psalm 16:8; Psalm 46).

- It is a realization that He wants His people to be aware of His presence and that He loves us. Seeking Him is an active pursuit that His Spirit helps us to accomplish.

This wording would have reminded the Hebrew believers of the Aaronic blessing and God's powerful love for them that comes not only with His presence, but with His favour. This seeking of His face yields power and peace as an overflow of His presence.

Jerry Bridges said, "true revival will occur when God's people are conscious of His presence in all of their lives", or to use this language: when they constantly seek His face.

4. Turn From Their Wicked Ways

When God's people enter the presence of God, their lives can be seen much more clearly for what they are. Just as when something is brought into the light it can be seen more clearly, so one's life when seen in the light of the face of God can be perceived more plainly.

The closer we get to God the further away we realize we are in terms of our own value and worth outside of the work of Christ. The more people see His holiness as they grow closer to Him, the more they hate their own sin, and realize its depth and depravity.

A turning from wicked ways is a call to repentance from sin, and a savouring of His forgiveness.

Turning from should always include a turning to, and the order in this prayer includes a seeking of the face of God followed by a turning from sin.

The more satisfaction the follower of God gets in their walk with God the less they will drink from the cisterns of sin that hold no water.[4]

One of the reasons a grasp of the gospel is so important is that when followers of God grow in intimacy with God, their realization of need for His grace increases! If you are truly seeking revival as you pray, please do so actively starting with you and your own heart.

---

4. Jeremiah 2:12–13

I love the statement, "if you want revival, draw a circle around yourself and ask God to start there."[5] So, personally and then corporately pray this! "Will you not revive us again, that your people may rejoice in you?" (Psalm 85:6)

---

5.   Rodney "Gipsy" Smith

Prayer

Father, I approach you today longing to know you more, and to experience your grace. I am your child, and rejoice that you love me and have called me to know you and follow your ways. I acknowledge that apart from you I can do nothing. My salvation, and my entire life is all of grace, and I do not deserve your lavish love, yet rejoice that you have given it to me. I am yours and weak, and yet you use weak people to accomplish your purpose. I have sinned. I fall short of your glory in thought, word and deed, and repent of that and ask that you would cleanse me and forgive me. I long to know you more and love you fully. I want to live in your presence, and have that keep me from sin, and cause me to have confidence in your power and presence.

I turn from my wicked ways, and I turn to you. Will you not revive me again and allow me to live my life conscious of your presence, defined by our relationship, and on mission for your glory!

Oh Father, take my life and use me to draw others to you, and accomplish what you desire and revive your church!

Take a moment to write this phrase Jesus taught His disciples to pray in your own words:

Prayer Notes

- Adoration: Focus on who God is: His attributes
- Confession: Agree with God on your sins and turn your back on them and your face toward Him.
- Thanksgiving: Start with the gospel and then thank Him for every good and perfect gift.
- Supplication: He wants to hear from your heart specific things you want Him to engage in.

8

Send Us

Then he said to his disciples, "The harvest is plentiful, but the laborers are few; therefore pray earnestly to the Lord of the harvest to send out laborers into his harvest." Matthew 9:37–38

It has been noted before that there are very few prayers for non-believers in the Bible. In fact a careful study yields one, and it is powerful (Romans 10:1), but many have asked why there are so many prayers for those who know Jesus and so few for those who don't.

I think the primary reason is relational—the focus of prayer is God's glory and conformity to His image. I also think that God's people who are mature live on mission for Him. Stated another way, God's people who know Him intimately live as labourers in the harvest.

One of the great treasures that occurs when God's people renew their devotion to Him is that they live on mission for Him, and He uses them in His sovereignty to bring His salvation to many.

Matthew 9:37–38 is a prayer request from Jesus to His disciples, and it is a prayer for workers, so that the harvest will be taken in. This is a prayer that God's people would live on mission for God's glory.

Jesus has compassion on the lost and hurting. In the direct context of this verse we find Him ministering effectively to their physical needs, but His love does not stop there, He longs for them to know the *Good Shepherd*.

So this is a prayer that those who know Jesus as their Shepherd should pray, not only as an offering of their own lives to Him to live on mission, but also that the church would scatter in the world, and be in the world but not of the world on mission for Him.

Literally, in the original, this could read: the Lord who is harvesting, pray for His children to go and harvest…what He is bringing in. It should give His children confidence in sharing their faith, and a deep desire to pray this, and to pursue this with their lives. This is a prayer for global missions, but more specifically this is a prayer for God's people to live on mission in the communities where He has placed them.

If you are a child of God, you are one of the labourers sent into His harvest and privileged to be His tool to bring people into a relationship with Him through sharing and living the gospel.

Prayer

Father, you are at work in the world around us and in the lives of those who don't know you. You have chosen in your perfect will people who are Your very own. I pray that we as your church would be faithful to share who you are and what you have done, that we would live in the world, but not of the world, and that each of us as labourers would take seriously Your call to work in Your fields. Father, I am willing—please open my eyes to see reality as you want me to, and help me to share your gospel with those you have chosen to harvest through me. Please use our church to see eternity changed, and to draw people to yourself!

Take a moment to write your understanding and answer to this prayer request that Jesus gave to us as His disciples.

Prayer Notes
- Who do you believe God might have chosen to reach through you?
- Pray specifically for them: that they would have open eyes and respond to Jesus through the drawing of His Holy Spirit.
- Pray for yourself and others: that you would faithfully live and share with them in a way that brings the Lord's harvest in through your labour.
- Plan: Make sure you take some time after you finish praying to make a plan that includes how you will live your life as an ambassador for God.
- Reflect on 2 Corinthians 5:11–21 as you do this.
- Adoration: Focus on who God is: His attributes
- Confession: Agree with God on your sins and turn your back on them and your face toward Him.
- Thanksgiving: Start with the gospel and then thank Him for every good and perfect gift.
- Supplication: He wants to hear from your heart specific things you want Him to engage in.

9

Patterns of Prayer

Pattern of Summer Prayer Meetings at Cloverdale Baptist Church

- Read Matthew 6:8–15

- Review:

- God's Word: (10 minutes)

- Time in prayer: follow through on pattern

- Requests:
  › For the Bride
  › Shared
  › For the harvest

Other Helpful Patterns

Throughout history it has been helpful for Christians to follow patterns of prayer to help them focus on things that are Biblical, relational and right. They are dangerous in that they can become mindless repetition. To avoid that, if you are following a pattern, be sure to engage your brain! The oldest one I am aware of is the *A.C.T.S.* pattern:

A.C.T.S.

A: **Adoration:** *Give God praise for who He is*

This is usually a focus on His attributes, and seeks to acknowledge with the heart who He is. It is one of the ways to keep prayer confident, relational and focused. It is helpful to remember who the follower of Jesus is approaching so they can be reverent and confident in this relationship. Beginning here also is a help in focusing prayers on God's glory, and escaping a cultural predisposition to man-centredness.

There are many good books on the attributes of God, my favourite is Tozer's *Knowledge of the Holy*, and his helpful quote is a good one to remember as you enter into God's presence:

> What comes into our minds when we think about God is the most important thing about us. The history of mankind will probably show that no people has ever risen above its religion, and man's spiritual history will positively demonstrate that no religion has ever been greater than its idea of God. Worship is pure or base as the worshiper entertains high or low thoughts of God. For this reason the gravest question before the Church is always God Himself, and the most portentous fact about any man is not what he at a given time may say or do, but what he in his deep heart conceives God to be like. We tend by a secret law of the soul to move toward our mental image of God. This is true not only of the individual Christian, but of the company of Christians that composes the Church. Always the most revealing thing about the Church is her idea of God.[1]

Knowing God by J.I. Packer is another excellent resource when seeking to develop a biblical view of who God is and what He has done.

Take a moment to brainstorm on your own or with others the attributes of God, and try to include with them the places in the Bible that He describes Himself in this way. It might be helpful for those seeking to grow in their prayer life to keep an ever growing list as they read the Bible at other times, and grow in their knowledge of God.

---

1. Packer, J. I. *Knowledge of the Holy.*

The Attributes of God: *Brainstorming List*

Attribute:	*Text*:
• God is *holy holy holy*. This means He is utterly separate and absolutely pure.	• Isaiah 6 • Revelation 4
• God is *sovereign* This means that He is in control of all things, and working at all times to accomplish His will.	• Ephesians 1:11; Job 1:21–22; 2:10; Psalm 115:3

Another way of getting to know God better is to look at the descriptors He uses for His *name*. These are almost always tied to displaying something about who He is, and worth learning and using to drive this time of *adoration*.

- Elohim—strong One, divine (Genesis 1:1)
- Adonai—Lord, indicating a Master-to-servant relationship (Exodus 4:10, 13)
- El Elyon—Most High, the strongest One (Genesis 14:20)
- El Roi—the strong One who sees (Genesis 16:13)
- El Shaddai—Almighty God (Genesis 17:1)
- El Olam—Everlasting God (Isaiah 40:28)
- Yahweh—Lord, "I Am", meaning the eternal self-existent God (Exodus 3:13–14).

Remember that your goal is to know Him as He has revealed Himself, so continue to grow in this and seek to keep it from being mindless repetition. As you grow in relational prayer, your understanding of who God is will also grow, and you will discover an ever-deepening and defining relationship with *Him*.

C: Confession

This is taking the time to agree with God, particularly about your sin. It is helpful to confess sins to one another, it is essential to confess sins to God. This is an opportunity to agree with Him about your sins, so it includes repenting, or changing your mind and behaviour. 1 John 1:9 is helpful in promising that He is faithful and just to forgive our sins and cleanse completely, and it is a relational experience of our justification reality.

Some patterns place this step in prayer ahead of adoration, (C.A.S.T.) because of the Scriptures that claim that if we have sin in our lives our prayers are hindered , however I have found in my own experience that time reflecting with God on who God is, is the best way for me to see myself as I am.

There are two ditches to avoid in this time of confession, the first is a flippancy towards sin. God hates sin, and sin is dangerous in the life of a follower of God as it steals their joy, hinders their mission, and damages their walk with God. Sin is serious, and should be taken seriously. The other ditch to avoid when it comes to confession is not experiencing God's forgiveness. His grace is greater than any sin, so all sin that is truly confessed to Him can and will be forgiven. In fact the great reality of the authentic Christian is that their sin has already been dealt with by Jesus on the cross, and their condemnation removed (Romans 8:1), perhaps even more wonderful, if that is possible, Jesus' righteousness is given to them.

So, with hatred towards your sin, and wonder towards your Savior, take the time to agree with Him about your sin, rejoice in His forgiveness and heal your relationship with Him!

Take a moment to ask God to search you and know you, to see Him as He is, yourself as you are, and embrace His forgiveness.

> Search me, O God, and know my heart!
>   Try me and know my thoughts!
> And see if there be any grievous way in me,
>   and lead me in the way everlasting!
> (Psalm 139:23–24)

As you do this, remember that sin is in thought, motive and deed, and can even include not doing the good you ought.

T: Thanksgiving

The follower of Jesus is called to be thankful always. The only way to do this is to keep the gospel central and constantly in mind. Adoration focuses on praising God for who He is, thanksgiving focuses on thanking God for what He has done.

Thanksgiving for the follower of Jesus includes all of His good and perfect gifts, and this can and should be ever growing, *but* its focus and depth will be on what Jesus has done for them on the cross.

It is helpful to preach the gospel to yourself every day, and include in that a deep and heartfelt thanks, and to keep a list of things that Jesus has done for you personally in your life, and through your life for which you are thankful. Take a moment, and in your own words (use personal pronouns), write out what Jesus did for you, in the context of what you deserved.

Thank you Jesus for your gospel. Take a moment and reflect on other things that you are thankful to God for. Remember nothing is too small to notice, or reflect on as you thank Him for what He has done.

S: Supplications

This is where followers of God present their requests to Him, knowing that He hears them and loves them. This can include everything and anything, and the deeper the follower of Jesus grows the more reflective of the biblical prayer requests they will be.

> Rejoice in the Lord always; again I will say, rejoice. Let your reasonableness be known to everyone. The Lord is at hand; do not be anxious about anything, but in everything by prayer and supplication with thanksgiving let your requests be made known to God. And the peace of God, which surpasses all understanding, will guard your hearts and your minds in Christ Jesus. (Philippians 4:4–7)

> Humble yourselves, therefore, under the mighty hand of God so that at the proper time he may exalt you, casting all your anxieties on him, because he cares for you. Be sober-minded; be watchful. Your adversary the devil prowls around like a roaring lion, seeking someone to devour. (1 Peter 5:6–8)

It is helpful to keep a list of the things that you are praying for and the answers that God is giving, not only to measure your own growth in prayer, but also so that you can add His answers to your praise items. Remember to look for the good in His answers that include *no*, or *wait*. Make a list now of things that are on your heart and mind as you reflect on your own life and ministry.[2] Try to include in your lists your own needs, the needs of your family and friends, your local church, and missions.

---

2. Carson's book on prayer, *Spiritual Reformation*, transformed my own supplication time as I now seek to match my requests to those that Paul, inspired by the Holy Spirit prayed. The pattern of the Lord's prayer is also particularly helpful in growing to know what to pray for.

Supplications:

I.O.U.S.

John Piper has been particularly helpful in giving me a guide using I.O.U.S. to keep my prayer time focused and biblical. The following is taken from an article at *desiringgod.org.*[3]

> In chapter nine of *When I Don't Desire God,* John Piper introduces a memorable and helpful acronym for what to pray before reading Scripture: I. O. U. S.
>
> - **I**ncline my heart to you, not to prideful gain or any false motive. (Psalm 119:36)
> - **O**pen my eyes to behold wonderful things in your Word. (Psalm 119:18)
> - **U**nite my heart to fear your name. (Psalm 86:11)
> - **S**atisfy me with your steadfast love. (Psalm 90:14)

An unfortunate side effect of repeatedly praying the same prayer is that, over a period of time, it can lose its sense of pertinence. One way to keep it fresh is to unpack the content with language that expresses what you mean in a new way.

For example, here's an amplification of the I. O. U. S. prayer:

- *Incline my heart to you, not to prideful gain or any false motive.* That is, focus my affections and desires upon you, and eradicate everything in me that would oppose such a focus.
- *Open my eyes to behold wonderful things in your Word.* That is, let your light shine and show me what you have willed to communicate through the biblical authors.
- *Unite my heart to fear your name.* That is, enthrall me with who you are.
- *Satisfy me with your steadfast love.* That is, fulfill me with the fact that your covenant love has been poured out on me through the death and resurrection of Jesus Christ.

---

3. Parnell, J. (2021, June 1). *One Way to Avoid Vain Repetition.* Desiring God. https://www.desiringgod.org/articles/one-way-to-avoid-vain-repetition.

L.O.V.E.

I am often asked what to pray for, in terms of the local church. Here is a pattern that I use to help focus my mind and heart. Key things to pray for our congregation:

- *Love Relationship with God:* Core of who we are (Matthew 12:28–31) That we would be a church that is relational, that experiences God's love, that makes the relationship which drives and defines everything else! That this love would be first, and that we would be relational Christians (Revelation 2:4).
- *One Heart and Mind:* (Romans 15:5–6; Philippians 1:27) Unity together for God's Glory! Division is one of the key tools of the demonic realm to attack the church. This is a passion for unity in the family that includes humility, the mind of Christ, and passion for His Word and mission.
- *Vision would be God's that we will pursue together:* Holiness, Truth, Mission, Love for the glory of God. (Philippians 1:21; Galatians 2:20; 1 Peter 1:16; John 17:17; 2 Timothy 3:16–17; Matthew 28:16–20: Ephesians 3:14–21; 1 Peter 4:8). This request is for the leadership of the church to understand God's plan for their specific church, and to communicate it in a way that can be shared and followed. It will always be a Great Command, Great Commission passion, and will include the particular preferred future that is God's will for that local church.
- *Eager Servants:* that we would be a church full of eager servants seeking God's glory together with all our might. (Ephesians 4:11–16; John 13:1–14)

In our consumer society it is easy to for those who attend a service to see themselves as fans, rather than fully devoted followers of Jesus. This is a prayer request that asks for God to help those who know Him to realize they are a part of His plan to help their church family conform to the image of Jesus, and to share the gospel in their community and world. Often in the Canadian culture, criticism has replaced engagement, and so this is a prayer that people would not only come to receive, but to serve.

Piper has a helpful article that seeks to display everything that the New Testament church prayed for. It is a good measurement tool to use against what you currently are praying for, and to guide your requests for yourself and others in the future:

What the New Testament Church Prayed For [4]

They called on God to vindicate his people in their cause.
And will not God vindicate his elect, who cry to him day and night? Will he delay long over them? (Luke 18:7).

They called on God to save unbelievers.
Brethren, my heart's desire and prayer to God for them is that they may be saved (Romans 10:1).

They called on God to direct the use of the sword.
Take the sword of the Spirit, which is the word of God, praying through all prayer and supplication on every occasion…(Ephesians 6:17–18)

They called on God for boldness in proclamation.
Pray at all times in the Spirit…and also for me, that utterance may be given me in opening my mouth boldly to proclaim the mystery of the gospel (Ephesians 6:18–19).
And now, Lord, look upon their threats, and grant to thy servants to speak thy word with all boldness (Acts 4:29).

They called on God for signs and wonders.
And now Lord…grant your servants to speak thy word with boldness… while you stretch out your hand to heal, and signs and wonders are performed through the name of thy holy servant Jesus (Acts 4:30).

---

4. Piper, J. (2021, June 1). *What the New Testament Church Prayed For*. Desiring God. https://www.desiringgod.org/articles/what-the-new-testament-church-prayed-for.

Elijah was a man of like nature with ourselves and he prayed fervently that it might not rain, and for three years and six months it did not rain on the earth. Then he prayed again and the heaven gave rain, and the earth brought forth its fruit (James 5:17–18).

They called on God for the healing of wounded comrades.
Let them pray over him, anointing him with oil in the name of the Lord, and the prayer of faith will save the sick man and the Lord will raise him up (James 5:14–15).

They called on God for the healing of unbelievers.
It happened that the father of Publius lay sick with fever and dysentery; and Paul visited him and prayed, and putting his hands on him healed him (Acts 28:8).

They called on God for the casting out of demons.
And he said to them, "This kind cannot be driven out by anything but prayer" (Mark 9:29).

They called on God for miraculous deliverances.
So Peter was kept in prison; but earnest prayer for him was made to God by the church…When he realized [he had been freed], he went to the house of Mary, the mother of John whose other name was Mark, where many were gathered together and were praying (Acts 12:5,12).
But about midnight Paul and Silas were praying and singing hymns to God, and the prisoners were listening to them, and suddenly there was a great earthquake (Acts 16:25–26).

They called on God for the raising of the dead.
But Peter put them all outside and knelt down and prayed; then turning to the body he said, "Tabitha, rise." And she opened her eyes, and when she saw Peter she sat up (Acts 9:40).

They called on God to supply his troops with necessities.
Give us this day our daily bread (Matthew 6:11).

They called on God for strategic wisdom.

If any of you lacks wisdom, let him ask God, who gives to all men generously and without reproaching, and it will be given him (James 1:5).

They called on God to establish leadership in the outposts.

And when they had appointed elders for them in every church, with prayer and fasting they committed them to the Lord in whom they believed (Acts 14:23).

They called on God to send out reinforcements.

Pray therefore the Lord of the harvest to send out laborers into his harvest (Matthew 9:38).

While they were worshiping the Lord and fasting, the Holy Spirit said, "Set apart for me Barnabas and Saul for the work to which I have called them." Then after fasting and praying they laid their hands on them and sent them off (Acts 13:2–3).

They called on God for the success of other missionaries.

I appeal to you, brethren, by our Lord Jesus Christ and by the love of the Spirit, to strive together with me in your prayers to God on my behalf, that I may be delivered from the unbelievers in Judea, and that my service for Jerusalem may be acceptable to the saints (Romans 15:30–31).

They called on God for unity and harmony in the ranks.

I do not pray for these only, but also for those who believe in me through their word, that they may all be one; even as thou, Father, art in me, and I in thee, that they also may be in us, so that the world may believe that thou hast sent me (John 17:20–21).

They called on God for the encouragement of togetherness.

[We are] praying earnestly night and day that we may see you face to face and supply what is lacking in your faith? (1 Thessalonians 3:10).

They called on God for a mind of discernment.

And it is my prayer that your love may abound more and more in knowledge and all discernment, so that you may approve what is excellent, and may be pure and blameless for the day of Christ (Philippians 1:9–10).

They called on God for a knowledge of his will.

And so, from the day we heard of it, we have not ceased to pray for you, asking that you may be filled with the knowledge of his will in all spiritual wisdom and understanding (Colossians 1:9).

They called on God to know him better.

[We have not ceased to pray for you to be] increasing in the knowledge of God (Colossians 1:10; cf. Ephesians 1:17).

They called on God for power to comprehend the love of Christ.

I bow my knees before the Father…that you may have power to comprehend with all the saints what is the breadth and length and height and depth and to know the love of Christ which surpasses knowledge (Ephesians 3:14,18).

They called on God for a deeper sense of assured hope.

I do not cease to give thanks for you, remembering you in my prayers… that you may know what is the hope to which he has called you, what are the riches of his glorious inheritance in the saints (Ephesians 1:16,18).

They called on God for strength and endurance.

[We have not ceased to pray for you to be] strengthened with all power, according to his glorious might, for all endurance and patience with joy (Colossians 1:11; cf. Ephesians 3:16).

They called on God for deeper sense of his power within them.

I do not cease to give thanks for you, remembering you in my prayers…that you may know…what is the immeasurable greatness of his power toward us who believe (Ephesians 1:16,19).

They called on God that their faith not be destroyed.
I have prayed for you that your faith may not fail; and when you have turned again, strengthen your brethren (Luke 22:32).

Watch at all times, praying that you may have strength to escape all these things that will take place, and to stand before the Son of man (Luke 21:36).

They called on God for greater faith.
Immediately the father of the child cried out and said, "I believe; help my unbelief!" (Mark 9:24; cf. Ephesians 3:17).

They called on God that they might not fall into temptation.
Lead us not into temptation (Matthew 6:13).
Watch and pray that you may not enter into temptation; the spirit indeed is willing, but the flesh is weak (Matthew 26:41).

They called on God that he would complete their resolves.
To this end we always pray for you, that our God may make you worthy of his call, and may fulfil every good resolve and work of faith by his power (2 Thessalonians 1:11).

They called on God that they would do good works.
[We have not ceased to pray for you that you] lead a life worthy of the Lord, fully pleasing to him, bearing fruit in every good work (Colossians 1:10).

They called on God for forgiveness of their sins.
Forgive us our debts as we forgive our debtors (Matthew 6:12).

They called on God for protection from the evil one.
Deliver us from evil (Matthew 6:13)

10

The Problem of Prayer

If God knows best, why pray? If God is sovereign and knows the future, why pray? Many Christians have this shared experience, "I have prayed and God did not answer my prayer in the way I longed for". There are many that I spend time with who are confused as to why God allowed their pain. The death of a child, the devastation of illness or accidents that leave pain and problems long beyond what we would allow for the children we love (Matthew 7:11).

If God has made us with free will, why pray? Does not the very idea of praying for someone hinder their free will? If God has a plan, or even if He knows the end from the beginning, why should I make the effort to learn how to pray, or take the time to passionately pray?

Is it ever right to express anger towards God over a situation? To be confused with unanswered prayer, or when God has said no to what we felt so strongly should have been a yes?

These are all worthwhile questions that many have asked me and others over years of ministry and real life in a broken world. Let me give the simple answers, all the while knowing that life is complex and eternity holds the answers that will satisfy the depth of the confusion.

The first and perhaps most important answer, that has already been given, is that prayer is relational. Prayer is the opportunity for children to approach their heavenly Father with life and experience His love and grace personally (Ephesians 3:14–21), and to bring change in their own lives because they have been in His presence.

Jesus knew the Father's will, and yet we find Him repeatedly in prayer, and even asking in full submission to take the cup of His wrath away, "nevertheless not my will but yours be done" (Luke 22:39–46). This was a relational prayer of intimacy that produced support and strength, and one that finds Jesus in full submission to the Father even when He knew what was coming was horrific!

Secondly we pray because it is a part of God's plan. God has chosen to use the prayers of His people, not only in His foreknowledge, but also specifically in space time history to accomplish what He desires. We have already noted that God is sovereign, and has chosen in His plan to use the prayers of His people to accomplish His will, even to change His mind if that were possible (Exodus 32:14). Prayer is relational, and a part of God's plan to accomplish His will for His glory.

Followers of God should also pray because God has commanded it, and because it is the cause used by God to move His power into a situation we are engaged in through prayer. We literally can join others in their struggle by praying for them (Romans 15:30). So we pray confidently that God will use our prayers to accomplish His will for His glory, confident that His eternal plan includes the use of the prayers of His people to accomplish His purposes. "God not only ordains the ends, He ordains the means to the ends."[1] We pray because we are His servants and want to follow Him fully.

Unanswered prayer is a problem that many Christians struggle with. They pray, they believe and yet it seems God does not answer. Over time most who follow Jesus come to the realization that He does answer all prayer, and that His answers are best and for the good of His children and the glory of His name. But sometimes, in the darkness of the moment, this is very difficult to work through when the answer is no, or wait. The most important help to the problem of unanswered prayer is relational,

---

1. Sproul, R.C. *The Prayer of the Lord.* Pg. 106

and a passion for a biblical view of God that ministers to the head and the heart (Job 42:1–6). When God's attributes of sovereignty, knowledge, wisdom, love and goodness explode together there is a realization that God can always be trusted, even, perhaps especially, in confusion (Romans 8:28–39). A follower of Jesus should also include in their view of life that they are not as wise or smart as God, and that their understanding is limited. Therefore there is a mystery of God's wisdom and love in the problems and pain of His children (James 1:2–4)[2] that can leave the follower of God confident, even when confused.

The question of prayer and the freedom of humans is a hard one to answer because both are couched in the modern understanding of those words. The Bible does not confuse the responsibility of humans to choose right and wrong and the sovereignty of God and His work in the life of humans (Philippians 2:12–13; Proverbs 21:1; Daniel 4:2–3, 34–35). This has been discussed for over 2000 years, and compatibilist freedom is helpful to understanding this and its impact on prayer and freedom.

God does not limit His freedom to the choices of humans (Psalm 115:3), and His plan is eternal and sovereign over choices people make (Ephesians 1:11; Acts 2:23; 4:27–28; Genesis 45:5–8; 50:20; Job 1:21–22; 2:10). The prayers of God's people are never limited by the choices those they are praying for make. Though every human is responsible for their choice, we rejoice that by God's grace, God-glorying choices can be made. Be encouraged to always pray and not give up, even for the most hardened hater of Christianity (Acts 9:1–19) for God is the One who gives the dead life (Ephesians 2:1–10). So pray confidently in the responsibility of humans to seek God's face, and be responsible for their actions. Pray for the power of God knowing that He is the One who can change the hardest heart, and draw people to Himself. He is the One who directs the king's heart[3], and can be trusted to use the prayers of His people to change eternity.

The question of expressing anger towards God, or others in prayer is an interesting one, given the precatory Psalms. The simple answer to what

---

2. Leith Anderson's book, *Praying to the God You Can Trust*, has been very helpful to me in explaining to my own heart the mystery of unanswered prayers.
3. Proverbs 21:1

is appropriate to share with God, and what is not, is that God knows how we feel, so praying to Him honestly is never a bad thing.

However, when we realize who we are and who God is, any feelings of entitlement or anger towards God will disappear (Job 42:1–6). It is always right to share your heart with God, but never okay to do it without realizing who God is and who you are. That should lead to confident rest from all anxiety as we cast our cares on Him (Philippians 4:5–6). So, pour out your heart to God, and as you do so, make sure the depth of your understanding of who He has revealed Himself to be is ever increasing. As we mature, we will discover less angst and anxiety and more rest and radical faith. That said, Job, David, and many others cried out to God in heart breaking honesty.

It is impossible to be angry with God when your heart is filled with thanksgiving that He loved you enough to send His Son to die in your place, and that through faith in Him you can be forgiven and experience eternal life. It is impossible to be angry with God if the gospel dominates your thinking. In fact it is impossible not to be *joyful* and *thankful* when the gospel is experienced. So if you are struggling, be honest with God, and pour your heart out to Him, even as you realize that, the closer to Him you grow, the less these feelings will be manifest in your heart.

As Tozer has so aptly said, "what comes into your mind when you think about God is the most important thing about you"[4]. This is as true in prayer as it is in the rest of life. So the better one knows God, the healthier and more effective their prayer life will be. Although many of their questions will not be answered, they will approach the throne of grace with confidence and find help in their time of need.

---

4.   Tozer, A. W. *Knowledge of the Holy.*

11

The Pursuit a Prayer-Filled Life

Prayer is something that works. Prayer is something that we should pursue because of the promises and stories in Scripture. Prayer is also something that God expects and commands.

Most Christians I know realize that their prayer life is deficient, and long to be better at it. My own life has been one where I have struggled with this, and longed to be one who lives a life of prayer, praying always, and having consistent times away for prayer. It is still something I am learning and growing in.

How can we be people who pray always and are growing in our intimacy with God so that our prayer life is developing?

1. Keep It Relational

Always remember that prayer is much more than a discipline, it is an expression of devotion, and a longing for deeper intimacy. One of the reasons that we struggle as Christians to pray is that we have slipped into a cultural lethargy that sees God as a small vending machine, to be pursued when we need a chocolate bar, rather than the creator and sustainer of the universe who loves us!

When seeking to improve our prayer life, it is helpful to remember the goal is not more prayer, but more of God. Not a better religion, but a deeper relationship. Christianity at its core is relational, and prayer a significant part of growing this relationship.

2. Keep Jesus in Sight

I love John MacArthur's perspective on what it means to pray continually: "praying at all times simply means an ongoing awareness of God—seeing every experience of life in relation to Him."[1]

This is definitely similar to keeping it relational, but it is the Psalm 16:8 reminder that Jesus is with us always, and we need never fear or have anxiety. This is the arrow prayer of Nehemiah as he was talking to the King. This is the heart of Paul as he lives all of His life in God's presence. Jerry Bridges once shared with me that the key to revival was living consciously in the presence of God. This is also the key to continual prayer, constant dependence, and courageous living. No matter what comes against you, if you know God is with you, you can face it with contentment. Practicing the presence of Jesus can also help you pursue obedience and purity in all areas, but that is another book.

If you want to learn to pray more, find ways to keep Jesus constantly in sight. This will also help your prayers to be made in faith, because instead of a discipline, or words you know you need to say to be a "good Christian", they become the cry of a heart close to the God of the Bible.

3. Keep Growing in Community

One of the best ways to learn how to pray well is to be around others who know God intimately and display it in their prayer life. Find people you want to be like because they are like Jesus, and try to be around them as much as you can. Learn to pray from them, pray with them, and as you grow, teach others to pray. Praying in community is not only biblical, it

---

1.   MacArthur, John, *Spiritual Boot Camp*. Pg. 31

creates a culture for learning how to pray more effectively. Find yourself some prayer partners that you can learn from, and when you have learned, some that learn from you. Personal prayer grows best in the greenhouse of community.

4. Keep God's Word Close

We have tried to do that with working through Jesus' teaching on prayer, but there is so much more. Carson's book is amazing in terms of working through the prayers of Paul, and if you really have a passion for learning, Rosscup's four volume set on the prayers of the Bible will help saturate you in this.

Having recommended books about prayers in the Bible, the most important way to pray is to actually be in the Bible, and read it as a relational book. Let it not only drive you to learn from the prayers that the Holy Spirit inspires, but also to drive your heart to prayer. God's Word is the best guide and grower of prayer. So go to Him, listen to Him as you read His Word, and respond with your heart filled with praise, thanksgiving, repentance and petition!

5. Keep Praying Even When You Don't Feel Like It

Carson calls this "praying until you pray"[2], and it is the willingness to fight through tiredness, apathy, or blocks. Keep praying, keep pursuing a life of prayer, even when it feels dry and hopeless. Carson pulls this idea from the Puritans, and he writes, "What they meant is that Christians should pray long enough and honestly enough, at a single session, to get past the feeling of formalism and unreality that attends not a little praying. We are especially prone to such feelings when we pray for only a few minutes, rushing to be done with a mere duty"[3]

It takes discipline to develop a healthy prayer life, even as we depend on relationship and the power of the Holy Spirit to produce this desire and discipline. Choose to pray, and keep on praying, even when you don't feel like it.

---

2. Carson, D.A. *Praying with Paul: A Call to Spiritual Reformation*
3. Carson, D.A., *A Call to Spiritual Reformation:*. Pg. 36

6. Keep It Personal

As much as you can learn from other people you are an individual, and a little unique. Therefore find ways that drive you to prayer, and use them for the season when they are helpful to you personally as you continue to learn from others how to live dependently in the presence of the Living God. Things that have helped me:

Prayer Lists: I have carried around prayers for my children, prayers for my wife, prayers for missionaries, prayers for those in my community. I know of some people whose lists are strategic, and each day has a different focus. I find this overwhelming and so avoid it, but keep my lists with me and growing. Even when you love someone, you might forget to pray for them, or for specific needs. So keeping lists helps you to stay focused, and has the joyful side benefit of seeing the amazing ways that God answers prayer.

Journaling: Joseph Stowell has a great book titled *Following Christ*. In it he allows some of his spiritual giants to share how they grow in their walk with God. Every one of them journals. Reading this I tried to journal, but have found it way to personal, so instead, I now journal using my own short form, and it has been a *huge* blessing to me. This format keeps me focused, allows me to know what I have prayed for, and lets me stay in prayer for long periods of time. I used to struggle praying with fixed attention for more than five minutes, and the journaling tool has allowed me to stay focused for hours at a time, with relational intimacy growing through it. Other than those I mentor, I know of no one who uses this style of journaling. So, I suggest you find what helps you and make it personal to what works for you, and accomplishes your desire to relate more intimately with God and impact more people for His Kingdom.

Patterns That Help: Really this book has been about patterns, learning from the Lord's Prayer. It is worth repeating—find patterns that engage your mind and heart, and learn from them.

In particular, Carson's book on prayer transformed my own prayer life, but Donald Whitney's stuff is also very helpful for my own heart and praying through the Psalms, as well as smaller books on the Lord's prayer including Sproul's, Mohler's, and so many more. Learn what God's Word has to say about prayer, learn how people pray, and follow helpful patterns you find.

There are also many other patterns people have followed. Find some that engage your heart and mind and use them, always being careful not to slip into mindless repetition, but finding your way to communicate to God from your heart.

Plans to Pray: I have found that if I don't set aside time to pray, the busyness of life crowds out what is the most impactful thing I could do: pray.

I have seen some people's plans, and although they are amazing, they overwhelm me, so again this is personal. For me, having a set time, and a set place is helpful, and when I miss those plans, it jars me. Routine and plans are helpful, but again, it is essential to reiterate, prayer is relational, not simply a religious discipline. So in your planning, keep the reminders that focus your life.

I have also found it helpful to plan into your daily schedule what I call symbolic prayers. These are prayers at meals, or before services, or when you know you will be short of time for prayer. In this you are acknowledging God's presence, seeking His Person and power, and then moving to action (or eating). Make sure you know when these "symbolic" prayers are taking place, and you undergird them with significant times of prayer, or you will find your spiritual life and ministry anemic.

Because prayer is so personal, it is important to develop a personal plan that will ignite your own prayer life. I have sought to share a few things that have ignited mine, and I hope they are helpful in engaging your heart and voice to God.

12

The Power of Prayer in Jesus' Name

The Bible promises us that anything we ask in Jesus' Name, we will receive. If all of God's promises are yes and amen, that is a pretty special thing! So, if this is our encouragement and faith-engaging promise from God, it is helpful to know what Jesus means.

What does it mean to pray in Jesus' name? For most of us it is the way we end our prayers, almost like saying, finally done. "Bless this food to our bodies' use, *in-jesus-name-amen.*"

It is a little dangerous to pray thoughtlessly, perhaps even more so to include the name of Jesus without thinking it through carefully. John 14:13 contains a precious promise, "Whatever you ask in my name, this I will do, that the Father may be glorified in the Son."

What does it mean than to ask things in Jesus' name?

We are supposed to be saying that everything we prayed for was offered in Jesus' name, for His honor and purposes. When we pray in Jesus' name, we pray for His sake more than our own…the final phrase of our prayer reminds us, as well as commits us, to submit all our requests to the glory of Jesus.[1]

Bryan Chapell in his great book on this subject, *Praying Backwards*, challenges the Christian to pray backwards, meaning to put Jesus' name first, so that you align all of the requests to follow with who He is. Simply put, to pray in Jesus' name means that we align ourselves with who He is. When the Bible uses the concept of name, it is referring to who a person is. To pray in Jesus' name is to align ourselves with His purposes and to pursue His glory, to acknowledge and rejoice in who He is, to align ourselves with Him in full faith, and to be prayer-filled with that relational focus.

Perhaps 1 John 5:14–15 helps clarify this so that it becomes a definer of our prayers more than a religious way of saying we are finished praying:

And this is the confidence that we have toward him, that if we ask anything according to his will he hears us. And if we know that he hears us in whatever we ask, we know that we have the requests that we have asked of him. (1 John 5:14–15)

Praying in Jesus' Name means we align our prayers with who He is and what He wants, and submit to His will fully and freely! I hope you will go buy Chapell's book on *Praying Backwards* if this interests you, as it develops this concept very well. Praying should be in Jesus' Name, at its start, in its passionate content, and in full submission at the end. So turn your in-jesus-name-amen, into *in Jesus' Name…*

---

1.   Chapell, Bryan. *Praying Backwards.* Pg. 13

13

A Plan for Sharing
the Gospel

It is essential to pray for workers for the harvest, as this book has called you to do, in response to Jesus' call, and as you do this, it is essential to prepare to be an answer to your own prayer.

How can you be ready to share with any and all who ask you about your walk with God? How can you be a worker in the harvest? Be available, for God has a plan to use you to show people how great He is (Ephesians 2:10).

Be aware of the best way in your own culture to share the greatness of this good news. Get the gospel right, live it, keep it in sight, and share it!

Keeping the Gospel in your Testimony

Q: Are we supposed to be able to share our faith?
A: 1 Peter 3:15–16: "But in your hearts set apart Christ as Lord. Always be prepared to give an answer to everyone who asks you to give the reason for the hope that you have. But do this with gentleness and respect, keeping a clear conscience, so that those who speak maliciously against your good behavior in Christ may be ashamed of their slander."

Q: Is the gospel an important part of this sharing? Can we just talk about how we helped ourselves, or our Grandma helped us, or our friend, or our auto-mechanic, or, or, or…
A: 2 Corinthians 4:5: "For we do not preach ourselves, but Jesus Christ as Lord…"
1 Corinthians 1:23: "But we preach Christ crucified: a stumbling block to Jews and foolishness to Gentiles."

Q: How can I structure my testimony?
A: A straightforward way to structure your testimony is in three stages:

Before: Simply tell what your life was like before you surrendered to Christ. What were you searching for before coming to know Christ? What was the key problem, emotion, situation or attitude you were dealing with? What motivated you? What were your actions? How did you try to satisfy your inner needs? (Examples of inner needs are loneliness, fear of death, insecurity. Possible ways to fill those needs include work, money, drugs, relationships, sports, sex.)

How: How were you converted? Simply tell the events and circumstances that caused you to consider Christ as the solution to your searching. Take time to identify the steps that brought you to the point of trusting Christ. Where were you? What was happening at the time? What people or problems influenced your decision?

Since: How has your life in Christ made a difference? How has his forgiveness impacted you? How have your thoughts, attitudes and emotions changed? Share how Christ is meeting your needs and what a relationship with him means to you now.

Important Tips to Remember

- *Stick to the point.* Your conversion and new life in Christ should be the main point.
- *Be specific.* Include events, genuine feelings and personal insights that clarify your main point. This makes your testimony tangible—something others can relate to.
- *Be current.* Tell what is happening in your life with God now, today.
- *Be honest.* Don't exaggerate or dramatize your life for effect. The simple truth of what God has done in your life is all the Holy Spirit needs to convict others of their sin and convince them of his love and grace.

Things to Avoid

Stay away from "Christianese" phrases. These "foreign" or "churchy" words can alienate listeners and readers and keep them from identifying with your life.

Components of the Gospel to Include in Your Testimony

Based on the colours of the bracelet.

Gold: Focus on God and His *holiness* (God has no sin and is morally perfect, and set apart from everyone else. There is no one like Him)! Heaven is a place to rightly want to go. The gospel is God-centred! God is *holy, holy, holy.*

Black: But, we have a massive problem that we can't solve on our own. That is we have sin in our lives. This black bead represents our sin. The Bible says that all of us have sin. "For all have sinned and come short of the glory of God" (Romans 3:23). God does not allow any sin in heaven. So how can we get into heaven? We can't. God says the punishment of sin is death. Death is eternal separation from God in hell. "For the wages of sin is death." (Romans 6:23)

At this point you want people to understand that they have done wrong things and that these wrong things have broken their relationship with God, and they can't earn their way back—ever.

Red: This red bead symbolizes Christ's blood. When we accept His free gift of salvation God washes us with his blood.

God sent his Son, Jesus Christ to live a perfect life and die on the cross in our place so that we don't have to receive the punishment we deserve for our sins. Instead we can have His perfect obedience given to our account! To make our relationship with God right, what we have to do is believe in Jesus as our Lord and Savior, and accept what He did on the cross for us as our replacement for the punishment of sin. (2 Corinthians 5:21; Romans 10:9–10; Ephesians 2:8–10; John 3:16–17; Acts 4:12) When we authentically believe in Jesus as our Lord and Savior, this will include submission to Him as Lord and learning to follow Him with our lives.

At this point you want the people to understand what it means to believe, and follow. Please focus on the person of Jesus and what He has done for us. Repentance summarizes this concept well: a change of mind that impacts every area of life, a change of direction.

White: Once we believe, Jesus washes us with His blood we are pure. We are no longer black with sin, but we are clean like the white bead. Because God took our sin, when we die, God can let us into heaven because our sin is paid for by Jesus death on the cross.

The condemnation we deserve is taken by Him, and we can now have a right relationship with Him forever. (Romans 8:1; 1 Peter 2:24; John 1:12, 29; John 3:16)

Green: After we believe in Jesus as our Lord and Savior, we want to grow so that we can become closer to God. This green symbolizes growth much like the green grass grows. We can grow by reading the Bible, praying to God, going to church and learning to obey God in all of life (baptism and beyond). "But you dear friends build yourselves up in your most holy faith and pray in the Holy Spirit." (Jude 1:20)

14

Getting the Gospel Right

What is the Gospel?

We often talk about being gospel-centred, or gospel-focused. To understand how to build a culture that is honouring to God, it is essential that we understand, experience, and constantly bathe in the gospel. To begin this growth in being a gospel-centred culture, we must grasp what the gospel is. There are many in our world who use the term but don't understand or experience the transformation.

The gospel is literally, "the good news", and it is good because it addresses the deepest and most desperate need of humans. The Bible is clear that getting the gospel wrong is dangerous (Galatians 1:8–10) and leads to destruction.

It is very sad that there are some who think they are saved but are not (Matthew 7:21–27), and others who are saved by grace through faith but who are not living in the fullness of what the gospel daily provides.

To experience this good news, there are five realities that must be grasped, believed and then lived in light of in daily experience:

1. *Reality About God:* A rich experience of the gospel is God-centred and always includes a belief about who God is that matches how He has revealed Himself in His Word. There is only one true God, who is holy, and who made us in His image to worship Him. His holiness refers to His separateness from His creation and His absolute purity.

2. *Reality About Humans (me):* All humans have sinned (Romans 3:23) and in this we have separated ourselves from God and are placed under His righteous wrath. The wages of sin is death (Romans 6:23), and the only way for sinners to pay for sin is to spend eternity separated from God in hell.

3. *Love of God Displayed in Jesus:* God loved us so much that He, according to His eternal plan, sent Jesus, His only Son into the world. Jesus lived a perfect life, thus fulfilling the law in our place, then died on the cross in our place, thus taking on Himself the sins of those who believe in Him. He rose again from the dead. In so doing, He conquered sin and death and displayed that God accepted this sacrifice and His wrath against sinners who believe in Jesus has been fully exhausted.

4. *Response Demanded by God Through Grace:* God now calls on humans, by grace through faith to repent of their sins and trust in Jesus alone for forgiveness. This belief in Jesus alone, is a faith that saves. When humans believe they are forgiven and reconciled to God, this new relationship becomes the centre of their lives.

5. *Reconciliation and Freedom to Live For Him:* All who are saved by grace through faith are made new creations, and seek to live a life that is surrendered to the Lordship of Jesus and devoted to His glory. This pursuit of holiness is a progression that He helps believers to pursue. The Spirit-filled life will include a desire to never ignore so great a salvation.

Mark Dever summarizes it like this:

A good way to summarize this good news is to biblically unpack the words God, Man, Christ, Response.

1. God. God is the creator of all things (Gen. 1:1). He is perfectly holy, worthy of all worship, and will punish sin (1 John 1:5, Rev. 4:11, Rom. 2:5–8).

2. Man. All people, though created good, have become sinful by nature (Gen. 1:26–28, Ps. 51:5, Rom. 3:23). From birth, all people are alienated from God, hostile to God, and subject to the wrath of God (Eph. 2:1–3). 3. Christ. Jesus Christ, who is fully God and fully man, lived a sinless life, died on the cross to bear God's wrath in the place of all who would believe in him, and rose from the grave in order to give his people eternal life (John 1:1, 1 Tim. 2:5, Heb. 7:26, Rom. 3:21–26, 2 Cor. 5:21, 1 Cor. 15:20–22). 4. Response. God calls everyone everywhere to repent of their sins and trust in Christ in order to be saved (Mark 1:15, Acts 20:21, Rom. 10:9–10).[1]

The gospel is so simple that a child can understand it, and yet so profound that it will be something that those who know Jesus will spend eternity celebrating (Ephesians 2:7).

The realities of the gospel are amazing, and must be grasped, believed and experienced to be saved and to live a victorious Christian life. It is not enough to know them, or even to believe them, they must *never be neglected* (Hebrews 2:3). The best way to "escape" this danger is to preach the gospel to ourselves every day.

---

1. Some of this material has been adapted from *The Gospel and Personal Evangelism* by Mark Dever, p. 43) (https://www.9marks.org/answer/what-gospel/)

Books on Prayer

That Helped Me Engage More Effectively in Prayer

Carson, D.A. *Praying with Paul: A Call to Spiritual Reformation.*

Whitney, Donald. *Praying the Bible.*

Henderson, Daniel. *Transforming Prayer: How Everything Changes When You Seek God's Face.*

Miller, Paul. *A Praying Life: Connecting with God in a Distracting World.*

Hughes, Kent. *Abba Father: The Lord's Pattern for Prayer.*

Chapell, Bryan. *Praying Backwards: Transform Your Prayer Life by Beginning in Jesus' Name.*

Piper, John. *A Hunger for God.*

William Cowper is said to have stated, "Satan trembles when he sees the weakest saint upon his knees."

"When the devil sees a man or woman who really believes in prayer, he trembles as much as he ever did." (R.A. Torrey)

"True prayer is a way of life, not just for use in cases of emergency. Make it a habit, and when the need arises you will be in practice." (Billy Graham)

"Prayer lays hold of God's plan and becomes the link between his will and its accomplishment on earth. Amazing things happen, and we are given the privilege of being the channels of the Holy Spirit's prayer." (Elisabeth Elliot)

"True prayer is neither a mere mental exercise nor a vocal performance. It is far deeper than that — it is spiritual transaction with the Creator of Heaven and Earth." (Charles Spurgeon)

"Any concern too small to be turned into a prayer is too small to be made into a burden." (Corrie ten Boom)

"Prayer should not be regarded as a duty which must be performed, but rather as a privilege to be enjoyed, a rare delight that is always revealing some new beauty." (E.M. Bounds)

"A prayerless Christian is like a bus driver trying alone to push his bus out of a rut because he doesn't know Clark Kent is on board." (John Piper)

"He that lives a prayerless life, lives without God in the world" (Jonathan Edwards)

"The greatest tragedy of life is not unanswered prayer, but unoffered prayer." (F.B. Meyer)

"The one concern of the Devil is to keep Christians from praying. He fears nothing from our prayer-less studies, prayer-less work, and prayer-less religion. He laughs at our toil, mocks our wisdom, but trembles when we pray." (Samuel Chadwick)

"Believe me if a church does not pray, it is dead." (Charles Spurgeon)

Rejoice in the Lord always; again I will say, rejoice. Let your reasonableness be known to everyone. The Lord is at hand; do not be anxious about anything, but in everything by prayer and supplication with thanksgiving let your requests be made known to God. And the peace of God, which surpasses all understanding, will guard your hearts and your minds in Christ Jesus. (Philippians 4:4–7)

So, *pray!* Really. Learning is not enough. Now pray until you pray and keep praying!

Manufactured by Amazon.ca
Bolton, ON